FAILFECTION

FAILFECTION:
Life and Lessons

K. Ira

THANK You!

ISBN
978-1-7351604-2-9 Paperback
978-1-7351604-1-2 E-book
978-1-7351604-0-5 Audiobook

Cover photo by: Mark Arron Smith
Edited by: Krista Munster, Sharman Monroe
Narrated by: Jen Mary

This book is dedicated to those who struggle with something in life, to those who have been subjected to an injustice in any way and to those willing to persistently challenge their own beliefs.

Contents

PROLOGUE.

Life isn't always good. Many of us have had major life-changing failures, the type that don't ever completely go away. Many of us are in difficult situations that can't be escaped, like quicksand or a vortex spiraling down out of control. For the luckiest of us, we only have a never-ending number of obstacles to manage.

I've found that one of the primary ways to tackle these obstacles and difficulties is through accepting failure as an important part of the process, hence the name "Failfection."

Impossible and Perfection

Imagine you are the best in your field of endeavor. You have overcome the toughest obstacles. Some would say you're perfect. Are you? The champion who has achieved everything only has one direction to go.

If you're perfect, that means you have done everything humanly possible. You are complete. You have nothing else to learn and nothing else to overcome. It would be impossible to do anymore; that's the definition of perfect.

Interestingly enough, being at the lowest points in life, the worst situations are no different. In those situations, there is usually a belief that nothing more can be done. What's the point of trying? There are no more options. It is impossible to escape the situation.

Instead of believing there are no more options, accepting failure means we know there is always something else that can be learned, that it's possible to move forward just a little bit more.

Fail to Infinity

Something that is interesting in this world is the idea of infinity. It's in everything; we just don't normally think about it.

As kids, maybe we had an argument that went like this: I'm ten times better than you. Nuu-uuh, I'm a million times better than you. Nooo, I'm infinity times better than you! Well, I'm infinity plus one times better!

We instinctively know that we can always do just a little more, even if it's only a little. In between every goal is an infinite number of steps forward. Sometimes, we surpass or achieve the goal; sometimes, we don't. But in all cases, we can still keep moving forward just a little.

If it's not immediately apparent as to why, just think of how many numbers there are in between any two numbers or points. What is the first number between zero and one? We could start with .1, or .01 or .001. It doesn't matter the distance between the points; there is always an infinite number.

I like to see those small steps forward that don't seem to go anywhere as failures. We may not realize it, but every time we fail, we are moving forward, learning, growing in some way.

Life and Lessons

This book is a series of short takes on some of life's most difficult problems. Topics include adversity, personal development, interpersonal, day-to-day, and societal issues.

The content within is available on failfection.com in a non-curated form. Thank you for your support. I sincerely hope that you find something within that is thoughtful and useful.

ADVERSITY

"To exist in this world, we must contend with humiliation, broken dreams, sadness, and loss."
–David Goggins

Suicide: The Final Choice

He was always reassuring. If we needed something, we could always depend on him. He didn't talk much about his family life, but he could cook some serious blackened chicken on the grill. When work was getting tough, we'd ask him how he was doing. He'd always respond something like, "Oh, it's all good, just taking it one day at a time." One day, he called in saying he'd be late; he had some things to take care of at home. He seemed stressed but, in typical fashion, assured us everything was going to be ok. He never came in, though, so we figured it must have been a rough day. We didn't realize we wouldn't get to have that reassuring talk ever again. If only we could have helped; if we could have been that one glimmer of hope for him.

When we get to the point of having no other option but to take our own lives, when we are stuck in nothing but truly terrible situations, when we've assessed all the options and have no positive outcome, when we know NO ONE can really help us, when the emotional pain is stronger than any physical pain we've ever felt, we have to remember: We are blind and the mind holds our sight. So, FREEZE and feel out the next steps very, very carefully.

Decisions With No Sight

While we are the ultimate decision makers, we are making decisions based on what the mind is feeding us. We don't see for ourselves. What we see as options, as our situation, are assessments that are manifestations of our mind. These options are based on our decisions, yes, but the sea of information the mind is holding is immense. Look up from wherever we are and try to take in the amount of information contained in just one look. Focusing on a single object, we know that single object had an origin; it has a particular molecular makeup combined in a particular way. It can be used in various ways. It can relate to other objects we've seen like it. We can do things to interact with the object. It has shape, color, texture, temperature, weight, and so on. That's just one object. We have to think to come up with these characteristics.

We may think, "That information doesn't matter. It's not important." Why not? Who says what is important? Are we sure we'd never need that information? We'd never need to correlate something to a similar object? Are we holding that level of attention on every object in the room or every object that passes by? How did we know the characteristics without focusing on it? Did we deliberately do that to every object we've ever interacted with? How was this information stored and how did we retrieve the information?

This line of questioning serves a purpose. It allows us to see that we are, all day every day, taking in an extremely large amount of information. Our conscious, of course, isn't doing this, which is why it's hard to imagine the vastness. Our unconscious mind is doing this on our behalf. We can consciously crunch information but we can't hold all the information. We have to send requests to the mind to crunch it and provide feedback. We ultimately decide where to go based on what the mind tells us is there.

Driving in Multiple Directions

All the mind asks from us is that we tell it where to go, what to solve. It doesn't care where we tell it to go. If we want to override survival instincts, we can do that. The mind will bend to our will, but it will typically warn us if there's anything being overridden or ignored — conflict or obstacles.

It is easier said than done, of course. There is a vast amount of possibilities, and things that we want often represent different directions. The mind has to take us in the directions we identify, but while it's great at crunching information, it can't fix conflicts in our own goals or in the directions we are trying to get it to take us. It will try to drive in multiple directions at the same time, which doesn't work very well. It will keep trying, though all the while, it will tell us there is a conflict. It won't always be obvious what it is trying to tell us, but it is guaranteed to be in the form of some loud and sometimes extremely painful emotions.

Looking at it this way, painful and difficult emotions are likely a result of one of two things: 1) conflicts between our goals/directions or 2) obstacles in the way of our goals/directions. What this means is that whenever strong emotions are encountered, it's time to assess what it is we want because there is likely a problem with achieving it. Then we need to change our direction and eliminate the dissonance based on what we truly NEED, not what we want. We don't need someone to love us. We don't need to carry everyone's burden. We don't need to hurt ourselves or others. The earlier we change direction, the better our options will be. If we ignore our emotions, the options get worse until there aren't any real choices left. We won't be able to see the difference between needs and wants. As our options dwindle, the emotions will get more painful and our mind will scream to do something, to make something happen.

The Final Choice

We can't speak for those who are no longer with us, so it would be presumptuous to make assumptions about how they truly felt. But their mind identified the option to end their own life and of the options available, it was likely the one with the least amount of obstacles in the way, the shortest path to no more pain, the only path that could solve everything. It has the least amount of conflicts because when life is over, there are no conflicts, there are no more predictions, no more information to process, no more emotional pain. It all stops and so the final choice makes sense to someone stuck in the abyss.

When the final choice is made, the pain may start to subside as the mind acknowledges there are no more barriers. Life itself is no longer the goal; death is the goal. Some may feel resolved; others may still hold on to life just a little. There would still be warnings from the mind, but subtle like a whisper in comparison to the pain up until this point. Some emotion would represent the state of our internal conflict, maybe fear, maybe anxiety, maybe sadness, maybe all the above. These critical seconds of relief may seem to reinforce the decision, as if to speak out in agreement.

When the final choice is truly upon us, we've missed many signs. We've missed many of the chances to change our goals and directions. We've missed many chances to remove cognitive dissonance and change conflicting goals.

We have to see that we act in accordance with the viable options available to us. The viable options are being provided to us by the mind based on our experiences, based on information around us and our choices over time. If we've led ourselves into a corner mentally, it will be very difficult to escape when no options are available, when the emotional pain is excruciating. Saying "never give up" sounds nice, but when we don't see that as a viable option, when we don't see an end to the pain, the words are meaningless. When we look for a logical solution and find none, when we can't find an answer to our problems just the way we want it, we think it's impossible; that there are no options. We believe that any rational person in our shoes would agree. We only have one final option left — one final choice to make.

Even if that is all 100% true, even if all rational people in the same situation would choose to end their lives as well, there are other options.

Find Insanity

Insanity, not in a clinical sense, is doing things or believing things that are irrational. To someone who is about to take their own life, that decision isn't insane; it is a culmination of their situation plus their overall experiences and conflicts that have existed along the way. So, for those in the most extreme circumstances, who see no options, who see no other way out, nothing but impossibilities, we instead have to find insanity. We have to go insane. We have to create something that doesn't exist and is not rational to us and make it real.

Having faith is commonly associated with religion, but it is a similar mechanism to insanity (this is not a dig on religion). With faith, we can believe something without question, even if it has limited or no factual or observable roots. When there are no options, when extreme circumstances occur, there needs to be something that overrides the impossible. We need to reach into the depths of our imagination, find a light no matter how irrational it may seem and follow it out. Now is not the time for skepticism; that should have come and saved us well before we reached the final choice.

As kids, we seem to be much better at this. We can create an imaginary friend if we don't have any. We can imagine ourselves as flying when we can't walk. We do that to expand our options, to see possible in the impossible. As adults, we call this insanity and delusional. Yet it can serve a purpose. We can take an impossible situation and become delusional, making something feel possible anyway. This may sound extreme, but this is no more extreme than taking one's own life. It's no more extreme than setting goals and having no way of knowing if they are possible or not.

The ideal choice is to find new goals that aren't in conflict, goals that are unified and life-oriented, goals that last for our lifetime. However, when things are extreme, we may not be able to imagine that far ahead. When emotions are extreme and mostly negative, it may be difficult to imagine anything positive for that matter. So, we have to keep it simple for now, as realistic as possible but positive and just outside of our rational understanding. Something that gives us time to ask for help, even if we don't have time. Something that helps us understand that we can't fix everything. Something that helps us keep doing good things, knowing that they will eventually work out given enough time, years if need be.

Imagine that getting help is now a viable option. Imagine that getting out of this situation is a matter of changing directions. Imagine that the pain will go away as we remove the dissonance, as we sync up goals full of possibilities and rip apart the negative goals that have none.

If we have a hard time feeling like we can go insane, if we don't think we can imagine something impossible, try this: Imagine a dark blue goat, one with horns. Imagine it in the sky floating but looking like it's standing on clouds. Imagine this goat looking down, saying in a deep voice, "Find the possible in the impossible." Then, have it sing "Mary Had a Little Lamb."

I bet we all were easily able to imagine that, despite it sounding ridiculous. Now, we just have to imagine something else that is closer to reality, closer to our problems and closer and closer until it's believable.

Whenever we find ourselves feeling like there are no options or that taking our own life is an option at all, we must STOP. Go insane if need be and ask for help, even if it's impossible for them to help. Imagine it isn't. Don't stop asking for help and searching within ourselves until we see there is always another option and the possibility of a positive future. Whenever that positive future becomes impossible, go insane and make it possible by choosing to live.

Disclaimer. There are exceptions to everything. Of course, this is all theory and we haven't discussed drugs, addictions, substances, or mental conditions that can instigate suicidal thoughts, but regardless, our message stands.

National Suicide Prevention Hotline: 1-800-273-8255

R.I.P. Mike. If we could chat, I'd say I wish you would have shared how defeated you felt. I wish that maybe, just maybe, you could have read something like this or anything that resonated with you to give you hope. Sorry, bud. Please help these feelings reach anyone like you; help them chose life and see the possible in the impossible.

Rock Bottom and the Downward Spiral

You are waking up in an alleyway as the sounds of traffic and people moving about get louder. You found an inconspicuous area that kept you safe and allowed you some rest. You think about your situation, realizing things can spiral out of control in what seems like an instant. But it started probably more than a year ago.

You were stressing about a relationship problem and losing sleep consistently. As a result, you were late more often and when you were at work, your performance was clearly diminishing. Because of this and the strict work environment, you were fired. It took about three weeks or so to find a new job and as a result, you became a month behind on everything. You used credit cards to float. You wouldn't get paid for another two to three weeks due to being new in the payroll system.

The time it took to get your first check made you a total of two months behind on everything, including rent and you weren't making enough to catch up. The eviction notice was sent immediately after the first missed month. By that second month, the court date was set. You were thinking that you'd be able to catch up by the court date in another month by not paying any other bills and eating beans and rice.

Yet the final straw hits. Just after your first few weeks of work, a horrible setback occurs that isn't your fault this time; the company went bankrupt. They have to let most of the workers go, including you.

The Spiral

When you are struck with a series of tragic events and have landed in a predicament, you're in a hole and have to work three times as hard to get out. Often, along with it is a host of strong and debilitating emotions, especially when there are relationships involved. Facing this negative spiral, you just want to ball up into a corner and sleep the troubles and pain away.

The last thing you want to do is think about what you could have done, or how you are or are not responsible for your situation. Sadly enough, you have no choice. You must channel those negative emotions to get you through to the next phase.

The thing is, unfortunate events have a similar parallel to fortunate or positive events. They compound onto each other. Someone having a successful trend could easily keep swinging upward. We're always on the verge of a single simple mistake or random unfortunate event that could start that downward spiral.

Simply forgetting to change the oil in your car could result in a blown engine leading to not being able to get to work on time, to losing your job, to not being able to pay for child care or other bills, to having bad credit, to being slated for eviction, to taking an illegal job to get a quick win, to going to jail. For those in nice conditions, this sounds extreme, but the sad fact is, when living paycheck to paycheck, this isn't as far-fetched as it sounds. Something like this can happen in a couple of months with just a few bad decisions or events along the way.

This negative compounding effect is extremely dangerous and is likely how many of us get ourselves into these predicaments.

What Is Rock Bottom?

For those in homeless situations in a wealthy country, there is an extremely high possibility that the series of events that occurred could have been and can be overcome. You can't go a mile in any major US city without encountering a Help Wanted sign. A homeless person without any major mental conditions or drug addictions is likely not at rock bottom.

True rock bottom is mental conditions, disease, famine, war, drugs and impoverished societies. We can recover from anything else and we have very little reason not to break out of the negative spiral.

Yet, typically when we talk about rock bottom, we aren't using it in that extreme context. We are usually talking about our mental rock bottom—the point when we can't take anymore mentally or emotionally. Something gives, something breaks inside of us and we either change for the worse or change for the better.

The interesting thing about mental rock bottom is that it is very different for everyone. One person's rock bottom for change could be going to jail. For another, it could be almost dying. And for another, it could be having to live with their parents after moving out. It's all a matter of personal perspective.

Drowning in Emotional Chaos

Hitting rock bottom mentally is like drowning in emotional chaos. The thing is, with strong emotions, the body is screaming for something to happen. Why is it so often we make horrible, poor choices in these situations? I like to think of strong emotions like an alarm—what is an alarm actually telling you? A fire alarm is saying there might be a fire; it doesn't say how big or how bad the fire is. A security alarm is saying someone might be in the building that shouldn't be; it doesn't say if the person is armed and dangerous or not.

Our emotions ratchet up those alarms based on the importance of whatever the situation is to us. Since we have similar alarm systems, the real difference is the levels to which we are alerted. Losing a football game may send extremely high priority alarm signals for one person but may be completely absent of a signal for others.

The problem is, the bodily reactions to a high priority alarm are similar, whether it's losing a football game or losing a job. Fear of speaking in public has a similar bodily reaction to fear from being hunted by a killer ape. Of course, we typically have the ability to realize this and while we may be petrified, sweating and unable to think about anything other than the threat of being on stage, we won't typically run off and hide.

However, imagine if that fear was mixed with constant anger, sadness and disgust all at once? Plus, instead of a singular simple problem like being on stage and presenting, you have to figure out how you will get your bills paid, how you will have enough money for food and where you will live next. Then imagine having a family member or significant other also feeling emotional and having to interact or argue with them. Then add in a simple addiction—nicotine, alcohol, caffeine—and go a day without it. The emotional burden of all of those factors essentially becomes the same as cornering a wild animal.

Tame the Beast

Find a quiet place. Thinking sanely is the most difficult part since the emotions have been consistently bombarding you with various thoughts and feelings. If your mind is in chaos, remove yourself from any stimuli, go somewhere you can focus your thoughts and take a few minutes. We aren't trying to be a Zen master. We can't expect our emotions and thoughts to ever quiet down completely but taking no action for a couple of minutes should be enough for you to take the next real step.

Acknowledge the reasons for the emotions. Be sure to acknowledge and understand the reasons, not the actions the emotions are pushing you to take. This could make your emotions start to boil again, so take your time, remove blame and unnecessary pressure. This is solely to understand what is causing the emotional pain.

Introspect at least three levels deep. For those not used to introspection, often we focus on the symptoms or causes outside of our control. Instead, we want to focus on ways we can avoid the situations in the future, which ultimately can lead us to how to change our current situation. In our scenario, the first level: We got evicted because we lost our job twice and didn't pay rent for too many months. The second level: We didn't pay rent because we didn't have enough income to support our job losses, and when we did have one, it was too little to dig out of the hole. Third level: We lost our job once because we weren't getting enough sleep and were too preoccupied with relationship problems.

Find the light, the north star. Emotions are all about balance.

The negative emotions you've encountered should always have a light at the end of the tunnel. The north star is a way to always know how to navigate—some form of hope, whether it's a month, a year, or ten or more years away. This is the most important step of rock bottom. We can't find this light if we're jaded by chaotic emotions, if we haven't acknowledged our emotions and our responsibilities. If you cannot find a positive light, you will almost certainly sink, crash and burn. This is your lifeline. This is what you look to as you fight out of your predicament. If you cannot find it, quiet your mind and create it. Paint the ideal situation and use that as your light. If you can't see it, it's because you don't believe it is possible; break those chains. This is not an option. See the possible in the impossible.

Attack the problems. Once you've done those steps well, you are ready to attack the problems. Each one of the problems could take long amounts of time to resolve. As such, you have to plan things out so that you can get small victories to help you along the way and also so those problems that cause the most emotional chaos are addressed first. Prioritizing the problems you attack is imperative to breaking out of the spiral.

Don't fall victim to easy fixes. This is a step only to remind ourselves that we are in this position because life isn't easy. If there's an easy way out of your emotions, out of your predicament, it is almost guaranteed to have a lot of other risks involved. Now, this isn't to say never take chances, but you have to do it wisely, not when you are at rock bottom. Get out of the spiral first, get back on your feet from rock bottom. Learn the lessons from being there before even thinking about easy.

Repeat. The thing is, being at rock bottom will be a nightmare; it will be difficult. Getting through these steps is something you may have to do every single day for a long while.

You'll be handling extreme emotions until you get your bearings. There *will* be setbacks, so you'll have to take them in stride repeating this process until you are free.

Life Isn't Fair.

You will have to fight twice as hard as someone who isn't in a negative spiral. If you compare yourself to someone in an upward spiral, your situation will look ridiculously bleak, as if the whole world is against you. The hand we are dealt may not be fair and it's almost impossible to sugarcoat that unfortunate truth.

You may have to toil away for years to get out of a negative rut due to a bad life hand, whereas someone else could have been born into riches and doesn't have to worry about wiping their own butt. The thing is, getting stuck thinking about another's "perfect" situation is exactly the type of thinking that will keep you in the downward spiral.

"Life isn't fair. It's just fairer than death." – William Goldman

Trapped and Discontent

Being discontent comes in many forms. Despite things like the "no regrets" cliché, it's not reasonable to go through life and not be discontent at some point. Yet being discontent doesn't necessarily mean it's chronic or debilitating. Having credit card debt isn't necessarily going to make us depressed. Similarly, choosing to date someone we aren't compatible with can make us feel discontent, but if we break up and move on, things can be ok.

But what if we feel trapped in a relationship? For example, we rely on the partner to provide half the income. Or, what if our credit card debt is preventing us from taking a particular curriculum and achieving our professional goals?

The trapped issue seems to be a crucial factor in almost every depressed feeling (e.g., chronic discontent). If we didn't feel trapped, then we'd just move on and stop feeling depressed. Normally, regret would help us learn what not to do, and being discontent would help us change what we're currently doing. Yet, for some reason, sometimes we can't move on from the discontent feeling. There's something holding us back. We can typically identify various tangible reasons, such as not having the money or some extreme event that can never be forgotten; something always goes wrong. In those cases, logically, we just can't find any real options.

Break Up ... The Choices

In *Suicide: The Final Choice*, we talk about how our unconscious tends to crunch a lot of information on our behalf. The idea is that when the choices are easy, the unconscious can quickly bubble up the answer and there isn't much to deliberately think about. However, when the choices are complex, our unconscious gives us some leading information but then lets us figure out the rest.

In these tough situations, although there are always a seemingly infinite number of choices, the real choices can almost always be broken into the most general categories. For example, if our discontent is an incompatible relationship, we can always start with two options: 1) break up, or 2) don't break up.

Of course, that isn't all there is to it. We'd need to continue to split the choices again and again to see other possibilities. If we break up, for example, that means we will be poorer and possibly not able to pay for rent or live the same lifestyle. We may need to get roommates or file for bankruptcy. If we don't break up, we either accept that we won't be compatible or try to change that. Again and again, break the choices into the most basic forms until we come up with a path that feels right and possible.

There may be those times, however, that even breaking up the choices into the smallest details possible still isn't yielding a good answer. Then, most likely, either our ideas aren't well defined or are somehow in conflict. All of these ideas in our minds are rooted by our understanding and experiences.

Finding Our Roots

If we encounter a decision that can't seem to be divided into simple terms, then most likely, the choices have various roots or dependencies tied to other choices and issues. What that really means is we may have a problem connecting all the cognitive dots. For example, what if our partner's mother was also our boss and would immediately and definitely fire us if we broke up? And more extreme, what if we quit? Would the mother push our partner to break up with us?

In this case, our job and financial goals are strongly linked to our relationship, making the decision more complex; every "break up" versus "don't break up" would be linked to "keep job" versus "leave job" as well as the other cascading effects. The most complex of problems has a vast network of links just like this. Except, to make matters worse, the links aren't only these nice clear, tangible lines; they will inevitably also be more obscure.

Obscure Roots and Cognitive Dissonance

How are we defining things like "good partner" versus "bad partner" or "good son" versus "bad son"? There are an insane number of these concepts and if any one of these concepts is in conflict, then our whole decision-making process becomes very suspect.

If, for example, we believe that a good partner would never get a divorce, then that is ok as long as all the other items in our decision tree line up. If we believed that without any conflicting ideas or dissonance, then break-up wouldn't even be an option. We'd skip that option and go straight to other possibilities like couple's therapy or self-help.

Yet what if our partner was abusive? Now, we have a wrench thrown into the equation. Does a good partner truly need to stick through abuse? To move forward, we'd either eliminate the dissonance by changing our definition of a good partner or feel trapped because we cannot figure out a way to be both a good partner and not be discontent.

This is the simplest of examples. Life is rife with many more complexities than this, yet it seems that if we do not eliminate the dissonance, we can easily get trapped in ways we don't even realize.

Self-Confidence Isn't the Answer; It's the Result

The interesting thing is, we hear "be positive," "believe in yourself," and the like, but the truth of the matter is if we could all just "believe," then no one would have problems with their self-confidence. Of those who feel trapped, how many truly feel or can feel self-confident? Even if we do believe in ourselves, if this belief is in conflict with other deep-seated thoughts, then we're right back where we started.

The thing is, self-confidence may not be the answer to anything. It may be more of a result. If we solve cognitive dissonance, we naturally solve our ability to make tough decisions. If we solve our ability to make tough decisions, we naturally start to accomplish more. This results in confidence, which is really just a feeling of our own ability to accomplish things.

That means that if we take care of our cognitive roots by removing dissonance as much as possible and by adding knowledge and experience, our ability to make solid choices and escape the various obstacles life throws at us gets greater and greater.

The Dangerous Slope (or Cliff)

The primary danger when we take this plunge to find our cognitive roots and remove dissonance is that it will not be easy. We will be challenging our own beliefs and we will feel more lost than before we even started at times. We will feel the inclination to double down on some areas, making us overconfident and rigid in the areas we need to challenge the most. If we double down on the wrong thing, we can easily set ourselves up for a strange trajectory even if dissonance is generally taken care of.

With all that said, fight the trapped and discontent feelings by continuously resolving dissonance and adding as much non-biased knowledge and experience as possible. The thing is, the solution may take a very long time. If, for example, we're in debt, we could be looking at years before things get better; that's a long time to be discontent. That means it is *crucial* to handle the long journey by getting satisfaction in the tiny wins along the way.

Burnt Out

Imagine you're working two jobs. Currently, both of them are at a point where everything is a fire, and everything is needed now. Not only is everything very fast-paced but you're also new at one of the jobs and so you're also learning their methods and processes. At the other job, you have a new boss imposing new requirements that seem impossible to meet. The first week was tough but now things have been very difficult and taxing for several weeks. You're tired. You're getting burnt out.

Opposite of Fun

Burn out is a funny thing. Typically, we use it to describe when we're working too hard but very rarely, if ever, to describe when we play too hard. There's something about the situations involved that make the difference between burnout and just another day. If we binge-watch our favorite series for hours on end, filling up an entire weekend, we won't typically feel stressed out (unless we're avoiding something). If we binge-play video games for days straight, all day and all night, similarly, we won't typically feel stressed. Yet, some of us have just one job and can feel burnt out like it's just too much.

What if instead of our favorite series, what if we were forced to binge-watch all the things we hate for hours at a time. Clearly, it would be difficult, and not only would it be not fun, it would start to get stressful if there was *no end in sight*.

Leading up to burn out, we are anxious and worrying about many things constantly. The problems, tasks, or situations are eating at us day in and day out. Our personal lives may even make things worse. This constant anxiety gets to a point where we burn out. We just can't take it anymore and we shut down.

Chronic Stress

Anxiety over extended periods is essentially chronic stress. Neuroscientists typically attribute burnout to chronic stress. The idea is that the body generates certain hormones when under stress and those hormones are ok for short bursts but are not meant to be the constant state. When under stress for long periods of time, the body starts to break down. For example, blood pressure increases, the immune system is weakened, muscle atrophies, digestion and metabolism change and we have difficulty getting good rest (which then causes even more problems).

Clearly, a large number of negative effects are associated with chronic stress. In fact, studies show that if chronic stress is encountered as a child, it can be correlated with childhood adversity and have life-long impacts on mental health and cognitive development. This is a silent killer and we should all be aware to help ourselves, our friends and families steer clear when possible.

Finding Balance

But how do we steer clear of chronic stress if we have to work two jobs to pay the bills? How do we steer clear of it if we want to do big things that will take lots of time and energy?

There's an old book called *Flow* by M. Csikszentmihalyi that explains that optimal experiences depend on having the right balance of challenge and our abilities or skills. When we have that balance, we can get into a state of "flow," and everything seems to work together without a lot of rumination about problems or anxiety about the task and we aren't bored to tears.

Finding the right balance that propels us forward without being chronically stressed can have a massive impact on our lives. We need to be self-aware to understand ourselves, what type of environment we thrive in and what type of environment we wither in.

Take a personality test. Find out about what makes us stressed to learn how to both manage the stress and target tasks and jobs that bring out flow. Bring out the best instead of bringing out the chronic stress.

Change the Changeable Goals and Beliefs

For some, politics, religion and other difficult areas are a massive source of chronic stress. In many cases, these areas require a change in mindset. Political beliefs in the U.S., for example, are almost divided in half. Anxiety over the half that doesn't agree is a recipe for chronic stress that will never get resolved.

As we've alluded to in other chapters, emotions tell us about our situation as it relates to our goals and beliefs. Studies have shown, for example, that random shocks give more anxiety than random shocks that we can stop with a press of a button, even though the length of the shock is no longer than it would take us to respond and press the button. It's a form of negative anticipation and rumination (beliefs) that causes anxiety.

To relieve stress in long-term, chronically stressful situations, we have a few options (assuming getting out of the situation is not an option):

1. Learn more about the stressors, about the details of why they make us feel this way. Often times, learning about all aspects of a subject and our anxieties can alleviate them because we find our assessments were not fully correct.

2. Increase our skills and abilities to handle the situation differently or better in some way. Along with learning about the subject, increasing our skills and abilities will increase our confidence with respect to the issue at hand and ideally get us closer to "flow."

3. Find our own "button" to release the pressure. If we've done our research, increased skills and find that our anxiety is still valid, then we should create our own button — something that can give us a sense of control over the situation. For example, for some, buying a weapon for protection makes them feel better and less anxious about increasing crime rates. Know, however, that this may or may not be a placebo and should be used sparingly. The better we understand, the better we can handle the stress. Or better yet, have it not turn into stress in the first place.

4. Learn to love it. This may feel like an exaggeration, but the point remains if we have to be in a situation, we

have to find solace in some aspect of the task, work, or situation. This is shown in the worst of scenarios. For example, prisoner of war survivor James Stockdale and holocaust survivor Victor Frankl both talk about finding something in their day to day life to look forward to without being unrealistic.

5. Always have a realistic end in sight. If none of the above aspects work, the last remaining option is we must have an end in sight. But it is imperative that the end be realistic. If we are unsure because it's too long, make the end many, many years from now on a horizon that we know is there but cannot see. As James Stockdale said, "You must never confuse faith that you will prevail in the end with the discipline to confront the most brutal facts of your current reality, whatever they might be."

Price of Success

Some say that to achieve great things, we have to work hard and hard work is going to be stressful, regardless, and that is the price of success. While this may be partially true, the real point that we all should come to understand is that chronic stress is in the mind; it's how we perceive our situation.

While it may be true that working hard is typically a prerequisite for financial success, that doesn't mean chronic stress is also a prerequisite. Just like binge-watching that favorite series, hard work can be like play if we have the right perspective and align our goals and our lives.

Remember, success doesn't necessarily mean we have to make a lot of money. It doesn't even mean we follow some grand passion. Success just means we have found a bit of flow in our lives; we found a path that is taking us toward wherever we ultimately want to go.

Dreams We Can't Achieve

You have a disfigurement or some form of obvious physical characteristic that isn't the societal norm. Yet you dream of being a model or some other dream that requires society to see your physical characteristics completely different than they do today. But every day, you are looked at sideways, called names by kids who may or may not know any better and treated like a disease or some charity case by society. Why can't society see your physical differences more positively? Should you give up on your dream of being a model?

The thing is, dreams (strong desires/passions/big goals) can affect our mental well-being. Having unrealistic desires can leave us unsatisfied with life. Yet curbing our desires also sets limits on what we could potentially accomplish. How do we know how far to set our sights? How do we know what we can and can't accomplish?

Is It a Dream? Or a Dream?

The first thing we have to understand is how badly do we want it. In many cases, dreams are just dreams, an imaginary world where we can go for solace or fun. For many of us, dreaming about being a millionaire is just fun, imagining what we would buy, where we would travel and what we would do.

But, we are willing to establish some dreams as a massive goal to fight for and accomplish. In both cases, dreams help us in some way. We have to decide for ourselves, however, if the dream is just a dream, or is there something about that dream we want to achieve?

Visualization -> Dream Meets Reality

The "Secret," visualizing and all the other self-help hoopla about thinking things into existence have some merits; they just do it in a barf-inducing way sometimes. When we visualize, we are essentially having realistic dreams through imagination. For example, there are studies of basketball players performing left-handed shots via practicing and those who have imagined how the shots should feel. Apparently, the visualization group did almost as well as the practicing group.

We won't take that to the bank but there are some other, more obvious connections with perception and imagination. When we catch a ball, for example, we are *imagining* the path of the ball before it gets to us to make the best decision.

If we create a complex, realistic visualization of how we can achieve our dreams, we are essentially planning. Yes, visualization is a fluffy word for planning in our minds. If we can't see the connection between reality and our dreams or end state, then we are missing important aspects and will have to think about whether our dream is reasonable or not. This doesn't mean we eliminate things that we think are impossible; it means we see a possible path toward the impossible.

If we have a disfiguration and can't see a reasonable way through hard work and smart planning to get on the cover of Vogue, then either we need to change our dream, or we're lacking in self-confidence and can't see other possibilities.

Self-Confidence

Ideally, we should understand the dream enough to know if it is realistic or not. But when we have low confidence, we may have an inability to understand what we actually can and can't do. The lower our self-confidence, the smaller our goals are to start. As we achieve smaller goals, our self-confidence will grow and we can tackle larger and larger goals.

We want to establish that without a shadow of a doubt: when we set a goal, we can tackle it. It doesn't matter how many times we fail; we have to build that confidence. If we don't have the confidence yet, we have to start smaller.

If we want to be popular but have a physical characteristic that is considered "not normal" for someone popular (and thus not confident), then we need to understand the details of what "popular" means to us and use those details as smaller goals. Instead of just the goal "be popular," how about getting one person at a time to like us? We'll find out if this is even a reasonable goal later.

Remove All Excuses

When we tell ourselves we're going to do something but then always have reasons we didn't or couldn't do it, we are cheating ourselves. We may think that we are confident, but if we have excuses for why we couldn't do something, then we may be confusing confidence with protecting our ego.

This is very dangerous because we can get stuck not achieving our goals, not moving forward, with constant reasons why we can't do something. Often, this will be accompanied by anxiety and possible depressed thoughts if it lingers too long.

As with self-confidence, we need to set smaller and smaller goals until there are no more excuses. If we truly believe there's a valid excuse to not achieve a goal, then why are we chasing that goal?

Meet Reality

There are times when we still want to achieve these big dreams but we have valid excuses, or our visualizations and planning determine our dreams just aren't realistic.

If we're four feet tall but want to dunk on a regulation ten-foot basketball hoop, that sounds unrealistic. What if we're sixty years old but want to be the fastest runner in history? What if we want to sing professionally but can't carry a tune? What if we want to be on the cover of Vogue but look like Shrek?

There are lots of things that we either have a major disadvantage with or there is no known possible way for us to do them. That is reality.

No Limit

However, setting limits on what is possible is not something that we do. It's not the Failfection way. We simply don't know. There's always infinity plus one. There was a time it was thought to be impossible to run a mile in under four minutes. The first person to break that time had to have "unrealistic" dreams. But somehow, they saw it as possible.

One of the best ways to stay in touch with reality is measuring our forward movement toward a goal. If we want to dunk, we figure we need a forty-five-inch vertical and are currently at twenty-five-inches. We need to see continuous improvement and measure ourselves against that goal.

When we no longer are improving, we have to change things up. This is the time most give up prematurely. When we are at this point, we have to truly know whether we have given it our all and attempted to adjust our methods of improving. If we ate, slept and breathed improving consistently for a year or more and still are not improving, then it is time to adjust fire and change up our goals or dreams. Of course, there is no real line in the sand but don't give up prematurely.

Journey > Finish Line

The right dream is one that emphasizes the journey while removing all limits. The person who broke the four-minute mile either thought it was possible or didn't think about that particular finish line. We need our dreams to be a never-ending sequence of goals—a way to point in a direction but have no finish line. As we mentioned before, a path to the impossible.

The dreams of being popular like Kendall Jenner, of dunking like LeBron James, of breaking a four-minute mile like Roger

Bannister, or of losing 100 pounds may be possible to some but not seem in the realm of possibility for others. But, in either case, they set forth a path that points in a particular direction. Whenever the dream starts to become a reality, we should start to dream new dreams pointing us in the next impossible direction.

Life Journey

If we've taken all of the areas discussed into consideration and we can't seem to find chasing our dreams fulfilling, there is a good chance it's not really our dream. Perhaps it's someone else's dream: our parents, our family, our mentor, our coach, our friends, our political group, our church, our society, the Jones, the popular person on Instagram, etc.

The never-ending list of influences we have on our lives cannot be stopped but at least we can control our interpretation of them.

The bottom line is that it's only natural that we don't achieve all our dreams. They are never-ending and when they do end, we should be creating another one. As long as they are our own dreams, our own path and no one else's, then we will find fulfillment in chasing them.

What We Can Learn from Illegal and Taboo Jobs

You're working online as a freelancer, as well as going to school. You have a professionally done photograph and always get compliments on it. Your family is poor, and you live in a poor country, but online, you are able to compete and provide services to anyone in the world. You've just started, so you only have a few jobs under your belt. It's difficult to compete with some of the more senior freelancers who've been doing it for a long time and have a large number of reviews and great ratings. Even still, a job you applied to last week, which appeared to be a perfect fit, could be in your hands. The client contacts you and says they'd like to schedule a video interview. You say sure, plan the time and get ready for what could be a long-term project. When the interview finally starts, you do well in the initial questions. At what seemed to be the end of the interview, the client says, "You are great! There's one more thing I'd like to ask. Would you mind changing into a swimsuit for me while I watch?" You are floored. You had not expected this at all. Before you hang up in frustration, the client says, "Look, I know this sounds crazy, but you can see my profile. I've done over $100,000 in expenses in the last month. I will pay you extremely well and this is only a one-time thing. I'll even pay you first."

In another situation, you are in high school. You live with your grandmother, who is retired, two cousins and a friend of the cousins in a small, two-bedroom apartment. Your cousins and the friend are clearly taking advantage of your grandmother. They also happen to be doing random drugs all the time. Your grandmother is very old and is starting to forget how to manage her social security money and pay rent and there's a threat of eviction. You try to get your cousins to pay something, but they don't care. They say they will live with their friend if they have to. You have to get enough money to pay rent fast, or you all will be evicted. You think to yourself that it would take a month before you can get enough money and by that time, we may get evicted. There's one thing you bet the cousins would pay for in a heartbeat: drugs. Their dealer visited the house regularly and would chat with you every now and then. The dealer knew you weren't into using, and when they found out about your financial situation, they asked if you wanted to be spotted a stash to try your hand at selling.

Situation + Normalization

Taboo and illegal jobs are jobs that people generally look down upon, but often, those in the professions somewhat "fall into" the jobs. It's not usually a grand plan that made them start down the path of these jobs. They aren't usually thinking, "Hmm, this is a great, perfect plan." It's often more of a situational thing. For example, if all around us is drugs, then doing them or becoming a dealer isn't a stretch at all, especially given the right situation; it's the norm.

Now, this does *not* excuse anyone who hurts another and there are those who seem to lack moral judgment. However, the right situation can call into question even the most developed moral code. Some people say they would never steal but have they ever been starving with a child? Others say they will never kill but have they ever been to war? The unfortunate truth is this moral gray area challenges us all the time in less extreme examples and is a reason for societal norms, laws and religions.

Confirmation Bias

Yet, we have to wonder, what is it that draws so many into these professions. Is it really easier or better to choose the taboo option if we accept the morality of it? In many cases, there is a good possibility that someone taking on a taboo job believes it to be the best option, but in reality, it simply isn't. In our drug dealing example, the high school student needs to find a quick way out of their eviction situation. While dealing could be a quick win, there are so many other factors that could become a problem and it could very easily become a horrible choice. If it is illegal, there's the law, there's the threat of theft or being attacked for product, the threat of getting into territory conflicts and the threat of the supplier getting arrested. In fact, we could argue that getting evicted would be better. The high school student is a minor and would be assigned to social services. The grandparent is a senior citizen and could likely get senior housing at a discounted rate. The cousins would get kicked out and live with their friend.

Given the right normalized situation, it is often difficult to see possibilities. This is likely due to confirmation bias, among other logical fallacies. We look at how the drug dealer we know is doing fine and is clearly well off. We look at the thought that eviction would mean we would be on the street with our grandparent with no way to make ends meet. The dealer said that it's easy and they've never had a problem. All of these things confirm the decision to become a drug dealer, yet in reality, it is all biased reasoning.

Those working in low-income countries are subject to our

freelancing example more often than may be realized by someone in a well-off country. For them, they only have to show a little skin or be extra nice online and these rich clients will send money over. It is an easy way to make money but again, their normalized situation has them in the confirmation bias spiral. While the situation of showing skin is easy and making money from it is also easy, there are plenty of downsides. Clients are less common, less marketable skills are built and it could be against the law or the policy of the freelancing organization, causing possible complications should anyone get reported. Entering a job with the caveat that skin may be shown and knowing these ramifications is a recipe for extortion in the future.

Accepting the Negative Possibilities

For an attractive person, it is easier than ever to make money and barely show any skin. And for dealers, savvy Internet knowledge can make it similarly easy to make money selling drugs. There are tons of other taboo or illegal jobs out there, and for those who truly acknowledge and accept the negative possibilities of the "taboo profession," it can be a logical way to make money and incorporate into bigger plans. Or, if the taboo profession is of actual interest, then that is, of course, their prerogative.

Yet there are very, *very* few situations that are truly more logical than choosing a legal and non-taboo profession. Not to mention, there is another very important mental side effect to the situation.

Reinforced Learning

The mental cost of taking on taboo jobs can be extremely high; it is a negative outcome that is not typically accounted for. When we accept these taboo jobs, we are reinforcing the ideas and beliefs surrounding the possibilities of the situation. We are telling our brains, simply by making the choice, that this is ok—this is the best way. We are accepting the mental burden of taking on something that is not a societal norm and carrying that weight mentally. Every time we take on the job, we reinforce the choices and biases and normalize the situation. As such, we are slowly hardening and closing our minds to other possibilities, all the while becoming subject to more anxiety and negative emotions.

This happens in reverse as well. Those who have performed non-taboo jobs for long periods can't even see the possibility of taking a taboo job or any reason they ever should or would. They can also become negatively biased toward those in taboo professions, labeling them as outcasts, or the "bad part" of society. Confirmation bias and all these other issues noted are common in all walks of life.

The Message

If we look down upon those in taboo jobs, we need to check ourselves; none of us are life's judge or jury. We may not fare well in similarly extreme life situations. For those in the taboo jobs, stay open to possibilities, always acknowledge and be able to spot non-taboo options. If we ever say it's not possible, then we are likely in some sort of cognitive bias spiral; if we are not, then seek help. No one in the history of humanity has survived without the assistance of someone else at some point in time. And no matter what, never, ever give up.

P.S.

Note, just to reiterate because it feels needed: This does *not* excuse anyone who hurts another, ever. Taboo and illegal work in our context are things that may be considered immoral but only refer to those who have no overt ill intent.

PERSONAL DEVELOPMENT

"If it falls your lot to be a street sweeper, sweep streets like Michelangelo painted pictures ... "
-Martin Luther King Jr.

Use This Rule to Improve

We have a tendency to assume that things aren't our fault when we don't achieve our goals or miss out on some opportunity. If we didn't get the job, we assume they must have had someone already in mind. If we didn't win the game, we remember that the refs were making some truly bad calls. What if we said that no matter what the situation is, no matter what the failure, no matter whose fault it is, the only way to improve is to prove ourselves wrong?

Questions Change Everything

Imagine a friend of ours applied and interviewed for a job but didn't get the job. They ask us, "What am I supposed to learn from this? I feel like it wasn't meant to be." With limited details, the amount that can be learned is also limited. If all we know is that they didn't get the job, we can only form very basic assumptions, such as "you must have done poorly in the interview," or "they must have had a better candidate."

But what if we get more information? What questions were asked in the interview? Was our friend able to answer all of the questions well? Did they know the subject of the job they were interviewing for? Did they talk to anyone who worked at the organization or for the group they were looking to work for prior to the interview? Were they on time, dressed in a way that best represented themselves? Did they get any feedback on the reasons?

All of the various questions start to dictate the information we ultimately learn from. It would follow then that asking the right questions can get us pretty far when we encounter any problem. But are we asking the right questions?

Wrong Questions

The important caveat is that whoever is coming up with the questions has a particular perspective and generally, it is one that suits the individual's best interest or goals. If the questions are biased or have a limited perspective, the answers, no matter how true they are, also are biased and have a limited perspective.

This is found in statistical studies all the time. Leading questions, loaded questions and a host of other biases can manipulate the results. For example, what if we asked, "Did the interviewer seem to be prejudiced? Was there anyone of the same race, gender, etc. represented? Wasn't there an article stating how bad the company was? Didn't your shoelace break right beforehand?" We could go on, asking questions that have less and less importance or more and more bias.

On one hand, there are no bad questions. But if we answer the first set of questions, we may glean some information about how we can improve or better posture ourselves for the next interview. The second set of questions could teach us that the interviewer was possibly prejudiced and the environment wasn't appropriate for us, that there were even signs pointing to the fact that we shouldn't take the job.

The trick to asking the right question is to simplify the question to be as broad as possible first, then let the answers dictate the next set of questions. So, if we are asking questions about race or gender, what is the broader question that encompasses that line of questioning? Most likely, this simplification will start to flush out broken or misguided questions. If our ultimate question isn't somehow aligning with self-improvement, then we know our intention isn't improvement.

Wrong Answers

Not only do we have to worry about the questions starting off as bad questions but we have to ensure that we can do something about wrong answers. Wrong answers could come from not doing enough research, making assumptions, or any other host of mistakes. There's nothing wrong with getting wrong answers; in fact, we should always expect wrong answers.

One way to do this is to use some lessons from science and treat our answers more like hypotheses and not assume our answers are definitely true. This means we have to formulate our answers in a way that uses disprovable statements. We have to have a method that can be attempted, which, if successful, will prove the statement wrong.

For example, if the answer to "Why didn't we get the job?" is "because the job interviewer was sexist," how do we disprove that statement? How would we prove that the interviewer is not sexist? If the interviewer said so, would that be enough? If the interviewer posted nice things about the opposite sex, would that be enough? Since the answer has no way of being disproved, it can't lead to valid conclusions.

This doesn't mean the answer isn't true; it just means we can't put the answer to the test. Without disprovable statements, our answers can become a dangerous safe haven for various logical fallacies and self-deception.

Self-Deception

What about when we intentionally (or unconsciously) answer wrongly? This may seem far-fetched, but it happens all the time. If we had asked ourselves after the interview, "Did we study enough before the interview?" our gut reaction may be, "Yes, of course, we did everything we could." The over-confident person is essentially practicing self-deception just the same as the person with low self-esteem.

Thankfully, disprovable statements can also help flush out self-deception. If the answer is disprovable, we can simply keep asking questions until we disprove it. So, for example, the statement "we did everything we could" is disprovable because we can at least try to come up with things we could have done instead. Find one thing and we would know we were wrong.

But wait. If we believe we can do something, isn't that a positive statement? Why would we want to try and prove it wrong? Put simply, we need to put it to the test; we have to find out if we're right or wrong. What is the point of believing something if we don't put it to the test? If we do happen to prove ourselves wrong, then we learn something and we also create a new statement to prove wrong, "We can't do it." Notice that if we always work to prove ourselves wrong, we will never be stuck in a rut. However, if we are always trying to prove ourselves right, one wrong belief could have us stuck forever.

The Learning Rule

Initially, I came up with the rule: ensure that the questions we ask ourselves always work together to help answer the ultimate question "How can I improve and be better prepared to accomplish the goal next time?" With this frame of mind, any set of questions could arguably be useful. The point was that by prioritizing the right question, all the rest of the questions and answers fall in line.

However, with more thought, I realized that there are a lot of skewed answers out there. There are those who wholeheartedly believe that they are improving themselves, yet somehow, they don't seem to be doing the right thing; their answers are somehow mired in possible self-deception or cognitive dissonance, and as such, their improvements and outcomes become more and more skewed.

So realistically, our concepts form a deceptively simple rule: **"Never stop proving yourself wrong."**

"We are trying to prove ourselves wrong as quickly as possible, because only in that way can we find progress." -Richard Feynman

Admitting to Being Wrong

You've argued your point, you're sure you are right and when anyone gives any counter-arguments, you shut them down or ignore them. They are wrong; what is the point of even entertaining what they are saying? And when there's the potential of being wrong, instead of understanding the counter-arguments, why is it so many of us have a tendency to "double down" and look for loopholes, excuses, or reasons to make our position make sense? Why are we so invested in being right?

Being Wrong

First off, what exactly is being wrong? Normally, we'd say, "Come on. Of course, everyone knows what being wrong means." But you all know better at this point. Let's use a physical example since it's the most obvious and easy to discuss. If a small ball bounced in front of us, we know what we saw. If someone said, "No, a ball didn't bounce right there," we'd say they were wrong; we saw the ball bounce with our own eyes.

What if the person who is saying a ball didn't land in front of us was right next to us when it happened? Now, we have two individuals believing two different things based on their firsthand experience. Barring lies, if this person truly believes there was no ball and we, of course, believe there was a ball, how do we resolve this normally simple problem?

Truth and Belief

Right and wrong are a matter of perspective that requires majority agreement in most cases. That may sound extreme because, as we know logically, there seems to always be an actual truth. What we have to realize is the vast majority of what we experience and hold as truths are actually more like beliefs.

Take, for example, when right or wrong is subjective and depends on not a single physical event but a variety of variables. It's easy to prove a ball landed in front of us if we had cameras (we won't get into deep fakes here). But how would we prove that a free market with international trade is better than tariffs to manipulate things? There are so many different variables that there could easily end up being a list of pros equal to a list of cons.

What this means is that being wrong can be proven only to the extent of what actually occurred, yet what actually occurred is filtered via our own observations and interpretation. What "actually occurred" is of course truth but what we "observed and interpreted" is belief that may happen to be true.

Another area that emphasizes truth versus belief is when our perception and reality don't match up exactly and we fill in the blanks automatically. For example, there is a natural blind spot in everyone's vision that is large enough to completely engulf a baseball if at the right distance and location in our field of vision. We don't see the blind spot. Instead, our minds fill in what "should" be there at all times. V.S. Rama-chandran, in his book, *Phantoms in the Brain,* discusses this and many other ways our minds have a tendency of convincing ourselves when we are trying to fill in details we don't have.

Partial Truths

This idea of convincing ourselves or filling in the blanks when we don't have all the information seems to happen all the time; it's only natural. We need to make assessments as to what to do with whatever information we have and usually don't have the luxury of waiting for perfect information every time. Essentially, we become masters at using only partial information to operate and get around day to day. The problem comes when we assume or turn this partial information this partial truth into the whole truth.

If we are running late for an important event and we hit bad traffic, how many of us will remember we were late before the traffic and how many of us instinctively think of the traffic as the whole truth? This is only a simple example; more complex examples can have a web of occurrences that could have us genuinely forgetting what the whole truth is.

This is a very slippery slope when someone can find true aspects and base their actions and beliefs on just a portion of what actually occurred while ignoring other portions (and fully believe it). If we've made a habit of doing this, of adapting truth to serve the results we are looking for, being wrong almost never happens. What would happen if then, at some point, we are challenged by someone as wrong?

Ego and Emotions

The need to be right, this investment to some psychologists, is the protection of our ego, the avoidance of bad things or bad feelings. We will fight to avoid the thought that "we are wrong" because if we're wrong, we're stupid or look stupid. Looking stupid comes with being teased or people not liking us. People not liking us could include our friends and family. If our friends and family don't like us, then it's as if we're outcasts. We wouldn't be able to have fun with them or have as many happy moments. Doom and gloom.

Of course, that seems like quite the stretch just from being wrong. There's likely some truth in it, though. Our emotions are built upon an extremely large amount of experiences. And, as we've alluded in other topics, emotions seem to be triggered based on our goals. It makes sense that we have to be right and make the right choice, and if we aren't, then we have something impeding our goals.

Even more so, however, is how we train our brains. Pathways in our brains are formed through persistent use. So a more simple answer could be that we fight being wrong because we are so used to convincing ourselves we are right. The emotions could be a result of that conflict.

Regardless of what the answer is, we should start to train ourselves to understand that making good choices is easier to do when we know more wrong answers; essentially, being wrong helps us be right.

Monty Hall Problem

An interesting way to drive this concept home is the infamous Monty Hall problem. "Suppose you're on a game show and you're given the choice of three doors. Behind one door is a car; behind the others are goats. You pick a door, say #1, and the host, who knows what's behind the doors, opens another door, say #3, which has a goat. He then says to you, "Do you want to change your pick to #2?" Is it to your advantage to switch your choice?"

Essentially, the important point is that obtaining the right information has an effect on the probability. We originally had a one in three chance to choose the right door, which means if we now know which door has a goat, we increase our chances to two in three by switching; we'd increase our chances to 50/50 if we flip a coin and we'd keep our original one in three chance if we don't change. The trick to understanding this problem is that the host has to know or eliminate two doors potentially, which gives us the two out of three chance. The host can't pick the car and can't pick our door.

This is a very counter-intuitive problem and being right versus wrong starts here. We have a hard time understanding how obtaining information can change a situation and, thus, our subsequent actions. In this case, the goat is like being wrong. By simply identifying one of the doors that are wrong, we have a much better chance of picking ultimately what is right.

All information that we uncover is adding to or changing various probability calculations. If we can compare ourselves briefly to artificial intelligence, the lesson is much more obvious; we have to increase probabilities through capturing as much information as possible. The more information we can obtain, the better we can tweak our results.

Accept the Possibilities

Ok, so hopefully, without even thinking about logic puzzles, we know that opening as many doors and understanding what is behind them is the best way to choose the right door. We get that truth is all about actual occurrences, and belief is the interpretation of those occurrences.

We also understand that actual occurrences aren't always directly observed; as such, we *have to depend* on other's observations and experiences. And when we are compiling all of that information, we typically only have part of the whole truth at any given time. With all these factors, it is only reasonable that there will always be disagreements on what is right or wrong.

Our part in this is to keep the ego and emotions in check and always accept the possibility that we are wrong; doing so will help us grow and maintain a sensible balance in this crazy world. Always remember, accepting the possibility of being wrong *requires action*; those who are excessively indecisive are no better than those who cannot accept being wrong.

Manage Anger by Doing This

You hop out of bed in a daze. The alarm didn't go off for some reason, so you have to rush to get ready for work. You sprint out of the house and know that you can make it on time. But if there are any delays at all, you'll be late. You know that this is the third time. That dang phone freezes in the middle of the night and doesn't start the alarm. You were going to buy a new one but never got around to it. Now there's a chance you'll get fired because it's the third strike.

As you make your way sprinting out of your house and to the street, you fail to look the opposite direction, not realizing someone is riding a scooter and you all crash into each other. It's not a horrible crash but both you and the rider are on the ground. As you apologize and get up to continue on to work, your phone is nowhere to be found! It must have flown out of your hand when you collided.

You frantically look around but can't find it. With no phone and no time to spare, you figure, "Screw it, I was due for an upgrade anyway" and take off sprinting without it. You get to work, and the manager says, "Sorry, you're one minute late. I told you that I didn't care and the next time you were late, I'm was going to have to let you go.". You look at the clock and it's only fifty seconds after actually ... which you explain but he's not hearing it. He says, "I'll have your last check sent to you when the pay period is up."

All you can see is red! You want to punch this guy so bad. This is ridiculous. If you knew he'd be that much of a !@#%, you would have just gotten coffee and called it a day.

Anger Is Asking for Something

When we are babies, we appear angry and cry when we want food. We are telling others that we want food, or at least that's what it seems. As such, when we think about emotions, we tend to emphasize social communication and interaction. Of course, this is reasonable but what we don't seem to do well is look into how we are communicating to ourselves with our emotions.

What purpose does it serve to be angry while we are a baby? Why would we instinctively get that emotion or what appears to be anger? We clearly want something, and we are clearly frustrated that we aren't getting it. The baby is kicking and screaming and seemingly exercising every movable limb. But what if anger's goal was to make us move, to force us to move toward the goal of getting food? It is speaking to us, telling us, "Hey, let's do something about this."

Now let's go back to our boss firing us after our Olympic efforts to make it on time without our phone. If our anger was talking to the boss, asking for something, what would it be saying? Aside from all types of obscenities, it's saying: "I want my job! You suck! I can't stand you! You shouldn't fire someone for being less than a minute late! You shouldn't fire someone who lost their phone and sprinted here anyway! You should be punched!"

Yet while the anger is telling the boss off, it's also screaming at you. "You need this job! How are you going to pay the bills? How the heck did you not see that person on the scooter? Why the heck didn't you replace that dang phone earlier? It's happened two other times; you should have had a backup! This is crap! You should kick him!"

Do you see the difference? Anger isn't simply irrational; it's asking us to do something about the situation and trying to force us to do something. Even though there could be extreme thoughts, there is something more behind those thoughts. Anger's purpose isn't to be mean or do mean things. It wants something more, just like the baby being angry and wanting food.

Memory Is Better When We Are Emotional

Now add the fact that there are plenty of studies out there that have found memories and various cognitive functions are stronger when they include heightened levels of emotion. Anger, in our example, is forcing us to remember this situation. It's engaging our memory of all things surrounding the situation. Why? Why would we want to remember such a crappy event and all the details that led up to it? Is it to remind ourselves why we should punch the boss someday? No. (Well, maybe.) Its purpose is to serve as a reminder, just like getting burned by a hot stove, to make sure we do something different next time and to learn from the situation. In our scenario, there are several things we could do to prevent this from happening in the future. Knowing the alarm didn't go off two other times and not having a backup alarm is like gambling. What for? Have a backup alarm. Plan ahead.

It's likely that most of us don't deliberately try to learn when we get emotional. We just bathe in the emotions without thinking, not realizing they are trying to tell us something more basic: "Please do something about this." All emotions, in my opinion, are trying to tell us that there's a problem or an event that our instincts want to do something about.

Managing Anger Is Solving Problems

Knowing that anger is there to remind us to do something is half the battle. But deciphering what our emotions are telling us and what our emotions want is the tough part. When a baby is kicking and screaming, she's saying, "Get attention! Kick! Punch! Scream! Solve this problem! DO SOMETHING!" But really, all she really wants is the problem solved: food. She wants to do something about her current situation; she wants to eat. The moment food is in front of her, she starts to calm down.

Now imagine that you are in front of that boss one last time. What the anger is highlighting is the fact that you want to be able to pay the bills, to keep the job and not have to worry about it. You want to not lose a job in this way again, even though the anger is also saying kick, punch, scream. If you convince the boss to let you keep your job, the anger would likely subside. But if you didn't, the anger would likely continue until you figure out a good, clear path forward. If you are still angry, even after identifying a clear path forward, most likely you haven't resolved the situation fully or found the real or only problem behind the anger.

Managing emotions (not controlling them) is a matter of always knowing they are simply there to help drive us to do something, to solve a problem. It's up to us to determine what that something is by listening and being self-aware. It's not easy because many times, the problems our emotions are asking us to solve are complex. If our emotions seem to be pointing in the wrong direction (if our anger seems to *only* want something negative or extreme, for example), then it's a sign that either we don't understand and/or we have ignored our emotions for way too long and the problems are too complex. The bottom line is to start listening and do something positive about it one step at a time.

P.S.

This is a touchy subject by definition. There are exceptions to every rule, so please seek professional help if your emotions are unmanageable, negative and extreme, or are causing problems despite your efforts.

Building and Sustaining Habits

You've been in a job that required getting up early and going to work on time at the same time for the last two years. You've never been an early bird or someone who's on time for personal events but you made sure to get there on time for the entire two years.

Now, however, you're no longer in that job and you're allowed to come in whenever you like. You decide you may as well stay in the habit and keep getting up early and be consistent. The first week is business as usual but you have to make a doctor's appointment. Normally, you'd schedule leave and take off to make the appointment but since there's flexibility in your new job, you schedule the doctor's appointment for first thing in the morning. Another week goes by and a friend is leaving the area and has a small late window to see you before they leave the next day. You decide to hang out knowing that you can go into work later if needed. Another week goes by and you have to go to a four-day conference that starts mid-morning.

After just a month, you realize you've started getting to work about 30 minutes later than you used to. What happened to that habit you formed for the last two years? Where is the precision that you were held to previously?

Fallible Habits

Have you ever forgotten to grab your keys, wallet, or another important item before you left home? After hundreds of times of not forgetting, well over 21 days, well over 300 days, you still manage to forget sometimes. Clearly, this habit thing isn't as infallible as we make it seem. What is causing these strange inconsistencies?

Imagine trying to change a serious addiction when we can't even fully control whether we remember our keys or not. Imagine trying to change our emotional response (road rage, anxiety, etc.) when we can't manage to get to work on time consistently.

The thing is, we treat habits as if they are infallible, as if, once we've made something habitual, it's in stone. It simply isn't. In fact, it can be argued that nothing in our minds is fixed permanently. This means that every habit is subject to being broken at the slightest change in your situation, which is typically called life.

To add to this problem, there is a degradation effect that occurs with just about everything in the known universe. For example, if we were to not work out and lay in bed all day every day, our muscles would atrophy. We'd become weaker, affecting just about everything in our life. No matter what herculean body we had and the habits we formed using it, by laying there consistently, everything gained previously will be lost, including those habits.

The Conditioning of a Habit

We love the idea of habits because we can make actions feel automatic. We can make them the norm and thereby continue to achieve whatever it is we ultimately want to achieve with less effort. The concept is to ingrain things into our minds through practice and repetition. If we want to enforce this even more, we add some rewards or punishment in the right way and create a conditioned response.

As most of us know, Pavlov developed the famed experiment of ringing a bell and serving food to a dog, resulting in the bell causing the dog to salivate before seeing any food. This classical conditioning underscores the idea of an expected reward or punishment, which governs our mood. By having an expectation of some reward or punishment, things change in our brains, just like the dog expecting food and salivating.

Pavlov also helped form the concept called reconditioning, showing that reconditioning can take form much faster than the initial conditioning. This means that the most ingrained, conditioned response can be reconditioned quickly given replacement stimulus.

If there is a correlation between habits and classical conditioning, it will make sense that a formed habit can be broken easier than it was originally made. That coincides with the idea that often replacing a habit with another habit is easier than removing the habit altogether.

Imagine if, instead of a single bell before getting food, we have a series of events. And instead of just relating food to these series of events, we relate getting paid, being socially accepted, staying healthy, etc. The point is we experience a never-ending list of stimuli and responses; they intermingle, become conditioned and get reconditioned non-stop.

The Solution: Never Stop

There is no secret or easy win. Every habit must be tended to consciously, deliberately and consistently. Thinking that something is a habit and you don't have to think about it is the same as saying you don't have to train. In sports, training to make something a habit doesn't mean you can stop training once they are habits. Things may feel a little easier when you build positive habits but it's not because you aren't putting effort into the habits.

If there is something we actually want to be a habit, then we have to accept that we have to say NO to everything else that impacts our desired habit; we cannot relax once it has become a norm. Breaking the habit takes one instant; forming the habit takes a non-stop, never-ending series of forward movement.

Good to Great by James Collins explains the concept of a flywheel. Imagine if you have a large flywheel that takes a lot of energy to move forward. The only way to get it moving is a long series of small pushes. Over time, as you constantly make small pushes, the flywheel will move faster and faster. That momentum is what Collins explained is necessary to go from good to great.

Habits are no different. No matter what habit you want to create, you must constantly tend to it, remove every barrier and ensure nothing stands in its way. The most important habits are often tough to create and may stay tough to maintain. Let's not get lulled into the belief that once we form a strong habit, we can lean on and depend on it without putting in consistent effort.

Can't Find Passion

You're toiling away at the most mind-numbing job that has nothing to do with anything you like. A few middle managers are fighting over the next big promotion using every chance they can to one-up the other or stab someone in the back secretly. The catch is, you make a great salary, but you can't stand the job. It's starting to make you be like those other middle managers. It's making you chronically annoyed, which isn't doing anything good for your psychological health. It bleeds into your personal life even though you have enough money to do things you want to do.

The problem is, the opposite situation can be worse: a job that you have a passion for but makes no money can leave you struggling to make ends meet, not being able to support your lifestyle, let alone a family. The stresses of worrying about the next bill or how to fix the broken car can be extremely difficult.

There are tons of polarized views on following your passion because it doesn't usually seem realistic. If our passion is to play video games, then chances are we aren't going to make much money, which means we won't be able to afford a place to stay, food, or whatever other comforts we may want or need.

Everyone knows this in general—that we have to be realistic,

or we'll be stuck making no money living in someone's basement or worse. We get paid to work because it's something
most of us wouldn't normally do for free. We will play video
games for free but most of us wouldn't shovel snow for free.
Then why does something feel off? Why do we always feel
pulled to chase our passions to find that ever-elusive "fulfillment"?

The Supernormal Exceptions

Our misconceptions grow as a result of the readily available
supernormal stimuli. These are exaggerations that we see in
everyday life that we instinctively react to. One famous study
involved mother birds with black-spotted eggs. When the sci-
entist used a marker and put bigger spots on the egg, the
mother birds would pay significantly more attention to the
egg with the darker, bigger spots.

Funny enough, this is our world with the Internet and social
media. We see the most beautiful, the most successful and the
happiest people in these short videos and images. The opposite is also the case. We see much more of the worst killings
and worst cases of people being horrible or idiotic. These are
all forms of supernormal stimuli. We see the most exaggerat-
ed versions of everyday life.

It doesn't help that it's so easy to fake a great life and tell ourselves that if we believe hard enough, it will come true. Smile
for the camera next to a mountain and we look like we're having the time of our life. Buy an expensive car and post it with
#thegoodlife and everyone thinks we're making good money.
We don't have to show that we are up to our ears in debt, or
that we are unhappy with our significant other, or hate our
jobs.

All we see are posts of happy and successful people that seem to love their lives (and subsequently, their jobs). We have no idea whether it is genuine or not. After seeing nothing but happy, successful people, it would only make sense that we'd conclude that to get there, we must find what we love to do, find that passion.

Elons in the Basement

There are probably at least a few Elons in basements around the world. These are smart genius-type people who are researching building things because they love to figure out things and want to make a positive impact. There are probably at least a few Bezos out there too, born into different situations, working in good, corporate positions right now.

Having a passion for engineering doesn't mean we'll be the next Elon Musk. It doesn't even mean we'll have a fun or enjoyable engineering job. In fact, maybe we don't even work as an engineer because we can't afford school. Instead, we're in a basement teaching ourselves to build robots using YouTube and Internet blogs.

A wealth of people spend many hours after work focusing on some random thing that they love and are not getting paid to do. They're just doing it because they have a passion for it. Will they be successful from their passion? Not necessarily but they are probably happier than most without a passion.

What Is Passion?

Passion is that strong feeling or enthusiasm to do something. Passion seems to represent a culmination of strong positive emotions driving us toward something. What we fail to understand is that we don't typically have passion for a job in the strictest sense. We have passion for something about the job. The job of being an NBA player includes giving interviews, addressing fans in a politically correct way and behaving appropriately off the court, among many other duties outside of playing basketball.

Most of those folks who advise against following your passion for work are making semantically similar statements about following your purpose or somehow having a life outside of work. They are downplaying passion but, in the end, if we don't have strong emotions driving us toward something, it doesn't seem to be a very fulfilling life.

So, despite the negative views on following your passion, we happen to be very big proponents of following passion. The reason, however, isn't because it will make us rich but because it only makes sense. Who wants to live life without any feelings of enthusiastic drive? Imagine doing work without having something that drives us to do it day in and day out; that would be mind-numbing.

Following passion doesn't mean we do it for a job. Since when is the job itself the reason we work? We work to achieve goals; some of us have jobs closely related to our goals (e.g., NBA player wanting to be the greatest basketball player), while others have highly unrelated jobs and goals (e.g., stockbroker wanting to be the greatest basketball player). We tend to be missing the point when we speak about passion and jobs.

What MAKES Passion?

Let's explore what makes up passion with just a touch more detail. We know that good feelings in the brain are a series of chemicals. We also know after reading *Manage Anger by Doing This*, that there's a good chance that emotions are telling us about our ultimate instinctive goals. In the most basic sense, when things are getting in the way, we feel generally negative emotions. When we start to see the light toward our goals, we generally get positive feelings.

Passion from an emotional perspective is that light. Happiness is that light. So, successfully chasing our goals can make us generally happier than not chasing our goals. In the book *Behave: The Biology of Humans at Our Best and Worst* by Robert Sapolsky, one of the studies he mentions shows that overall dopamine release in anticipation of getting something can often be more than the dopamine released after attaining whatever that something is. This supports the idea that a long journey can be much more rewarding than the end goal. This is the real point of following passion. It means we chase those life-long goals, such that we are always moving forward with small boosts of positive feelings along the way.

Establish Unyielding Goals

In conclusion, all we have to do is set unyielding goals and do our best to achieve them. That's what following our passion means. The problem is that most of us set goals but they are weak goals. They are either inconsistent or are in direct conflict with other things we want. For example, if we have a goal of stay in shape but hate working out more than the desire to stay in shape, then it's not an unyielding goal. When we work out, despite how much we hate it, then we know we have an unyielding goal. That's following passion.

Notice that following passion doesn't mean we'll love everything; in fact, we may hate everything about what we are doing at first. But the unyielding goal generates passion that tells us we will do this anyway. Believe it or not, when we consistently chase unyielding goals, we are teaching ourselves to keep chasing them.

Passion isn't something that is found; it is something that is created through pursuing goals persistently. The more we chase our goals, the stronger our passion will be. So, if we can't find our passion, then we can create our passion by establishing unyielding, life-long goals and doing everything in our power to tackle them.

Being Popular: When Being Yourself Fails

When we look at various social media sites and those posting in it, sometimes we can feel fakeness. It's "too nice" or "too happy" or "too empathetic" or "too perfect," almost as if many of us are trying to master how to balance being liked by as many people in our community as possible. Yet, when we don't do that, if we are just ourselves, we may not get the likes and interaction we are hoping for.

With social media like YouTube, for example, if we search "how to gain followers," one common theme is "high energy" and "be excited," which most of us can't do 24/7. We end up creating this persona that shows everyone this excited, high-energy side that we want to show while hiding the sides that we don't want to be shown. Some of us can separate these areas well or it fits naturally with who we are, while others may get tired trying too hard.

In business, this is no different. The same concepts are used to a maximum: focus on the product or service in a way that allows for the most followers, which they hope translates to the most profit. For a business that caters to a particular group or audience, the number one goal is to sell or market to that group. We are taught to create a product or service and tailor it to our audience. In fact, we shouldn't even choose to do a product or service that isn't marketable, doesn't have a big enough audience, or is a market already extremely saturated.

Businesses, however, are also taught to find a niche within markets to get access to areas that are otherwise overly saturated. These niches allow businesses to thrive with just enough audience for them to do well but small enough such that they won't get pushed out by larger businesses and higher competition. They essentially create a way to be popular by being their own niche.

Being Popular

Just like businesses, we're taught to do something that would make us popular. We should find something that we can shine in so people will like us. Do these things so we can find a good husband or wife. Build our resume so we can get a good job. It's almost a life-long sales job of getting someone to believe in us enough to hire us, be in a relationship with us, be our friend.

In social circles, traditionally, we seem to use big, sweeping general groups: wealthy, smart, athletic, pretty, funny, cool, religious, etc. Society and those we interact with are like extreme magnets that are constantly pulling us to fit in or pushing us to stand out. Being a part of the popular groups usually translates directly to our livelihood and to our success.

"Be yourself" is the cliché told to everyone who feels like they don't fit in. The idea is good, but it often just fails in execution if we happen to be someone who is outside of the popular groups. The unfortunate truth is that if we are not accepted in our society or culture, we will find it hard to navigate in life. We won't get jobs as easily, we won't find friends as easily, we won't find relationships as easily. But what if we don't agree with the masses? What if we don't fit in? Do we really need to wear a mask all the time?

Being Exposed

Things are changing. Those who are faking it to fit into a particular group are finding that it is becoming harder and harder to fake. Social media is on 24/7 and, as such, they have to try and be fake 24/7, which can be extremely difficult. They are getting exposed slowly.

A business is no different. A business that cares only about the bottom line will make mistakes that will get exposed. Ultimately, this should help flush out the fakeness, allow us to be free to be ourselves and maybe even not have to live a life marketing to others.

Yet something happens that is somewhat counter-intuitive as well. When a superstar influencer makes good content and then is exposed for doing something wrong or not in line with their audience, this exposure doesn't always amount to much. Instead of being exposed and losing large portions of their audience, it further increases their audience and the existing audience either forgives them or makes reasons as to why it must have happened or why it was ok.

This seems to be somewhat true for many large groups as well. When election time occurs, all sides fire against the other side. Most things that are exposed during these times are largely not taken seriously by anyone on the exposed side.

Social media and technology are underscoring time and again that the creator of good content and good ideas doesn't equal good person. We have often painted our heroes in a good light and written history to glorify the victor. It is no longer always possible to underscore the great things and downplay the bad. Despite the threat of being exposed, more and more, we're having to learn to accept the dichotomy of a crappy person being successful or doing cool things.

The Niche

The niche is something that is a small specialized section of the population; sometimes this could be seen as obscure. There is an extremely large number of niches. Anything can be a niche; the topic of cardboard can be a niche both in business and in things people like to talk about. For example, if we google cardboard or how it is made, we can see the topic gets thousands and thousands of pages and views. There is a niche for just about everything and every single one of us has niches that they love.

The Internet is somewhat redefining the term because what was traditionally obscure is now accessible to anyone. The numbers are all relative to the size of the population in question as it relates to other similar areas. So, there's no hard rule of what classifies as a niche. In the U.S., American football seems to have a large number of fans but if we compare it to the entire world of sports, it is small enough to be considered a niche even with millions of fans. Fans of the NY Giants American football team would be even smaller but even that itself still has more than a million fans.

Strength in numbers is a social dynamic that likely goes back to the caveman and cavewoman days. In a school, the handful of unpopular kids who aren't athletic, pretty and would rather read than socialize in the cafeteria with others had no numbers traditionally. They were easily misrepresented. This is no more; now, the most traditionally unpopular groups are represented by millions across the world. They are represented by millionaire and billionaire business owners. They have ways to connect with all of them.

Today, technology and the general state of most well-off countries allow people to live by themselves, communicate with everyone and survive just fine. The need to stay in large groups is becoming less and less important. Smaller subsets and tribes are being created all over the globe based on the millions of niches out there. This dynamic is allowing all of us a chance to be popular in our own way, just as it's allowing a vast number of new small businesses into the economy.

Online Versus Real Life

The only catch is that our interactions in real life versus our interactions in the online world haven't found a good balance with each other yet. For example, while racism plays no real role during most online business transactions (because we have no idea who we are talking to or dealing with), it can still exist in real life. Or vice versa, we will find an online troll that spews hateful talk and nasty social media comments every day; yet we won't encounter that same behavior as much in person.

In the same way, niches are great online and for businesses, but they haven't fully translated in real life. This is likely because our real-life perspective has much less context to draw from. If it's our first day in school in a class of 30 other students and they don't already know us, they have no context of who we are, what we like and don't like or what our niches are.

All they can see is what we physically look like and how we act. For many of us, that is enough to make sweeping generalizations. These sweeping generalizations turn into judgments or stereotypes that can become very negative, which is also likely where nasty things like racism and bullying get their roots. It's all somewhat naturally occurring because of the way we tend to generalize. Without full context, we cannot make sound generalizations.

The problem of generalizations will never go away in real life or online, but it is clear opportunities for popularity are much better in a globally connected world than in a disconnected one.

Follow Your Niche

Despite the chase to be in the large popular groups, being popular in niches will have more and more impact. The more we all embrace this concept, the more it will only be natural for the negative stereotypes to slowly dissipate. How would we maintain a racist attitude if we saw the positive niches in a particular race? Bullying wouldn't target the unpopular kid because that kid would have their own niches that others would acknowledge and support. When we see someone who we don't have context for, we will start to automatically look for context instead of passing immediate judgment.

This may seem far-fetched, but in a world of 24/7 exposure, for most of us, it only makes sense to stop trying to fit into groups we aren't really a part of. It will only end in either us being internally frustrated and conflicted or being exposed. The best idea is to stop chasing something we aren't. Our own niches are essentially filled with things we actually care about, things we enjoy not on the basis of someone else's interests. That sounds familiar, doesn't it? Be yourself.

Three Ways to Be More Original ... Or not?

There have been an estimated 100 billion or more people alive throughout the history of this earth. Each of these individuals had/have the ability to think and process large amounts of information. It's been estimated that we each have roughly 70,000 thoughts per day. Although this number has not been validated, nor will it likely ever be, let's use it as a hypothetical frame of reference. If we live an average of 71 years, that means we could have somewhere around 1.8 billion thoughts in our lifetime. So, trillions of thoughts have been circling around throughout human existence.

When we think of it that way, it seems like there is no way we'd ever have an original thought. We're just a speck in the massive thing called life. But, these minds of ours have some crazy abilities and are quite unique.

Unique Combinations

Let's start with the idea of random combinations (or permutations) to help bring context to the word unique. Three different colored dice with six sides have 6^3 (or two hundred and sixteen) possible permutations where ordering of the colors matter. Think of that like having six shirts, six pants and six pairs of shoes, and we can quickly see why picking clothes isn't easy for everyone. At a place like McDonald's, let's assume there's at least 10 of each main, side, drink and dessert option; that's at least 10^4 (or ten thousand choices). Making a simple lunch choice comes with taking into consideration ten thousand options without us even knowing it.

Using this concept, we can create a completely original combination of letters that can easily surpass the number of atoms in the universe in one paragraph. We can say with a pretty high level of confidence that this random combination of letters below has *never* been written before (for those listening, it's a random jumble of 209 upper and lowercase characters):

```
YnHmwYT  sNYHfXC  XTZo  QBntLzXJ  HaDYiE  AkpA
WnUNMsOj  puVx  hTqkQDy  WCAihWe  u  prqcgJ  eDS  k
EFuSl  hcduh  r  TUeH  bTso  uXi  XbgBDZQ  CiQlAMdj
FUAD  rJprK  iw  TxtHX1  d  Fjq  dFSVJLt  xioNi  JL
arYVoP  gHfseQ  hx  i  gyGjY  U  MIWs  iNgYL  U  YrOX
jNi  gAAeytx  Pv  yMGmDVb  a  kTg  asdEtG
```

Since we have 209 characters in this blurb and roughly seven bits per character, we get 2^{1463} possible permutations. It is said that the number of atoms in the universe is around 2^{256}. Going beyond that by several orders of magnitude is a ridiculous number of combinations.

Ok, Ok, Enough With the Numbers

So, what does that mean, aside from the fact that we just witnessed an original smattering of letters that have more possible combinations than the number of atoms in the universe? Great … now what? It's still not really original. It's just a unique combination of letters, just as most new articles or books are.

Being original, though, is supposed to capture concepts or

actions that haven't been done before or done to the same capacity. The smattering of letters in just this way may have never been done before but the concept has. But what about context? Has anyone associated random characters to being original? Probably. But if we think about ourselves, we are just like that random smattering of characters except we also have thoughts, concepts and take actions.

If we made the random words into a poem, that could be considered original thought. But has anyone made a poem from randomly created letters? Probably. Has anyone associated random characters of letters to notes with different pitches, frequency, etc. to make music? Probably. But if we created a different sounding beat that *people liked* by experimenting with these same letters, would that finally be original? It's so difficult to prove that it becomes comical to even try. So then what's the point?

Who created the first cell phone? Was it Eric Tigerstedt because he filed the first known patent for a pocket-sized phone? Or was it Motorola since they created the first known demonstration of a handheld phone? Who is to say someone else didn't create it before Eric or someone else didn't build it before Motorola? Once a concept or thought gets out, it can rapidly be incorporated into everyone else's thoughts and actions, immediately taking off with no real ability to determine the origin. The fate of a writer who likes to put their ideas out there will find other's taking those ideas and remixing them, sometimes without even knowing it.

If we can't prove what is or isn't truly original, then we have to depend on social credit or social acknowledgment. Edison arguably won social acknowledgment over most others as the pioneer of electricity in the U.S. but was he the original'? Was he even better? So, we can't prove originality very well because it depends on social credit and is *completely subjective*. So, what's the point of chasing originality? Before answering that, let's see if we can identify three ways to be more original.

Three Ways to Be Original

1. Study and work harder and smarter at an activity than everyone else. This one is self-explanatory. If we spend more time with an activity, we will naturally have more information about this activity and thus more opportunity to do things that others aren't doing. Trying to do this with pursuits that a large portion of the world is doing makes for a very tough time, so we should be sure we have a passion for it in that case.

2. Engage in an activity that very few are doing—the sport, cheese-rolling, or shin-kicking, for example. The number of people who have been involved in these undertakings may be so few that we may bring something original to the table just because our uniqueness has a much higher chance of shining.

3. Create something new by adding to something existing. Sticking to sports as our example, there are only around 10,000 sports in the books. Coming up with something new may not be as hard as it sounds if we **base it on what already exists**. Heck, let's do it right now. Let's strap an office chair to our butts and wear a rollerblade on one foot and a regular shoe on the other. We create a ball that is a mix between a rugby ball and a basketball to make a slightly lopsided basketball, so it bounces a little off. We can only touch the floor with our feet when dribbling but we can roll in the chair for as long as we want without dribbling. The court is about the size of half a basketball court and the rim is eight feet tall. We could play two on

two. We'll call it fail skate ball or FSB. Is our FSB sport original? Has anyone done that before? Maybe but the chances are lower each time we add something ridiculous to it. Let's add a light plastic bat in one hand, safety glasses and headgear and give points for smacking someone in the face with the plastic bat but only if we hit them while shooting. Being hit without shooting would mean a foul. Has anyone done this before? On and on, we can go.

There you have it: three ways to be more original. But what does this prove? Our fail skate ball may still use a ball and a hoop. Some would argue that building on something existing isn't really original. I disagree but as we established, being original requires either the all-knowing or completely subjective social acknowledgment.

Everything we learn is built on the backs of others. Every painting can arguably start with a single dot; everything else is built on top. Our ancestors had the proverbial dot for language and everything else that is human. That doesn't mean we can't be original. Cell phones, robots, satellites and space travel didn't exist. We add on to our body of knowledge and achievements slowly, steadily to the point where original thought happens by all of us all the time; we just can't recognize it as easily.

A Cliché Ending

We started off discussing a random bunch of characters and how being original involves something that hasn't been done before through unique thoughts, concepts or actions. Let's close this out. I think we can probably agree that, mathematically, each and every one of us is like those characters, very unique (let's just say more than $2^{3,000,000,000}$ based on the human genome). Except unlike those characters, our unique combination includes our way of thinking, our experiences, our very detailed nuances, which are all different and thus unique.

Yet if we are all so unique, why are our thoughts and actions so similar? Why don't they feel original? My theory is that we are built to generalize. We mimic each other as babies, and we are trained to socially interact with common structures (like language). If we didn't, we'd have too massive an amount of information to compare and wouldn't be able to interact. There are studies reducing the number of base emotions to four, yet we have more types of neurotransmitters than basic emotions (around seven types, with several in each type). We confine everything, including our own emotions, to very limited, generalized boxes and expect originality, which is based on other's opinions. Anyone who says we've already thought of everything is stuck inside these very same boxes. Think of all the ways we can combine words, concepts, ideas, emotions and actions just like we did with our random characters and it should become obvious — the possibilities are literally endless.

We are all original thinkers despite the similarities and it can be mathematically proven. So, what is the completely unoriginal bottom line? Instead of focusing on being original, just focus on being ourselves; it's the same thing anyway.

Eight Seconds to Willpower and Baselines

Traffic sucks. You're plodding along and get to an intersection. On the other side of the road, you notice a car in a place that isn't ideal. The flashers are on and the person is getting out, looking distraught. You look back to see your light is green and you proceed forward. Eight seconds is all it takes for our attention to wane as we focus on the next task or situation. What would it take for us to not lose attention and choose to help this random stranger? Maybe we never would. Maybe we would only if it was a more extreme circumstance.

Memory and Attention

There are tons of things that can happen in our minds in eight seconds, from feeling any emotion under the sun to predictions and assessments of events we are witnessing through all of our senses. We can listen to music, drive a car, talk on the phone, avoid pedestrians and analyze a distraught driver instantaneously, all in well under eight seconds. The number of things we are juggling at any given second is immense, even if we don't always realize it.

It doesn't help that short-term memory alone can be as small as 15 seconds, and based on YouTube and social media statistics, people tend to move on in a mere five seconds. It makes intuitive sense then that if we don't focus on something, we could lose it completely very quickly. Add in the various things we are juggling, and it can be as hard as memorizing a phone number with one look, we just can't hold too much at once. When we actually want to remember something, we need to hold our attention longer until it gets stored more permanently.

The decision to hold our attention and keep something in focus occurs automatically in a very dynamic cycle. The details of what happens in the brain are for the neuroscientists to answer. But there tends to be a cycle of attention alternating between priorities based on what we want, what our body/unconscious wants and based on anything that stands out (like a loud noise, for example). If we don't choose one way or another, the unconscious seems to choose for us.

The Optimal Unconscious Decision

In our scenario, we saw a distraught driver pulled over. We were at a light and they were on the opposite side of the road. In our quick assessment, it didn't appear that the person was in immediate danger. Since the car was on the opposite side of the road, we would have to do a U-turn and we were sure that someone would eventually help. The driver was a male that didn't seem like a threat, but strangers are strangers after all, so there should always be some level of caution. It wasn't extreme conditions and there was a service station within a mile. We aren't usually consciously thinking of all these details but our unconscious mind will serve us the options based on its quick assessment. What choices do we make?

In an instant, unless we have a good reason not to, whatever is the easiest, less-risky option would be the choice our unconscious would serve up and we probably wouldn't override that choice. We know that we could spend an eternity helping others and never get to our own problems if we don't have some filter. To make matters even more difficult, maybe we have a myriad of emotions that are bubbling up as well. Maybe we are late for an important meeting, or maybe we just got into an argument with someone. The unconscious crunches all these variables to serve up the optimal choice.

What if, despite all that, even though it doesn't make sense, we still want to make a particular choice? When we override what the unconscious serves up, we are going against all the normal options, all the feelings and emotions. We push to do something that most of our mind is made up not to do.

Enter Willpower

Famous studies on delayed gratification and studies on decision making generally allude to the existence of something that takes up our mental strength. If we really want ice cream but we decide not to get ice cream, we are using mental strength to do so. Subsequent decisions and choices can continue to degrade this mental strength until we simply have none left. This mental strength to make choices and decide against what we want is willpower. Yet, it's peculiar that what we want would take willpower at all, right? It seems that what we want based on our past experiences and choices (unconsciously), isn't necessarily what we want here and now (consciously). Whenever there is conflict that needs resolution before taking action, we seem to be using up mental strength or willpower to do so.

Why exactly something takes more or less willpower is, of course, unknown; however, it seems reasonable that the less we have to deliberate, think and de-conflict, the less willpower we need to use. As a simple example, imagine having to choose a meal from 10 unknown never-tasted-before foods. Taking the time to process all of them and make a choice would take longer and likely spend more mental energy than just flipping a coin.

If we override our optimal choices consistently, then the trend of those choices could become the new optimal choice, reducing our need for willpower. If we reduce the need for willpower, we can save it for when it matters instead of using it for not eating ice cream.

Despite those who feel we shouldn't depend on willpower, it isn't that we should or shouldn't; it's just that sometimes, we must. If we always listened to what our unconscious minds provide us, it would be like a permanent autopilot that would never be overridden. What would make us any different than a robot at that point? It's not reasonable to have a perfect solution for every life situation but what if we gave ourselves a checklist?

Pilot Checklist

What we are looking for is for our autopilot to do everything that we don't want to have to think about and if we want, we can override it at will. In an airplane, the pilot sets autopilot to take care of the details that have to be adjusted constantly, like the rudders for wind, speed and general direction so they can focus on more holistic problems like anticipated turbulence, sensors, or equipment failures and various other issues.

What if handling those holistic problems is difficult though? What if those problems require several steps or things to keep in mind? Pilots use a series of checklists to manage their tasks to make sure they remember what they should do or keep in mind. This is what we can establish for ourselves to help us take a load off of our willpower and make better thought-out decisions without spending as much time and effort thinking about them. We can't address all of life's nuances, so we need a checklist for our character as a whole.

Character Baselines (The Personal Code)

When we make quick decisions based on what our unconscious thinks is best, depending on how we've gone through life, our default decisions could seem pretty selfish. It's not that we are intentionally selfish; it's just that we aren't thinking about it and we have nothing preparing us for what to do. In the case of our initial scenario of a random stranger stuck on the side of the road, we weren't prepared to make a decision about it, so we just moved on. It is no different with the myriad of day-to-day encounters that we can't fully anticipate: when to engage with someone who is argumentative, how to react when we are cut off, whether to tell a friend we don't like something they did, what to do when we're in a group that is doing things we don't agree with.

We all have natural affinities toward things like being more or less likely to do what the rest of a group is doing or more or less likely to engage with an argumentative person. But, what is interesting is that we aren't always consistent unless we knowingly establish what we want to do or what we hold important. For instance, in the book *Predictably Irrational* by Dan Ariely, he speaks of studies involving students being tested for their affinity to cheat. The test allowed students to grade their own tests and turn them in themselves. It was found that most students, by default, would cheat provided a simple, unintrusive, easy option. However, it was also found that those who were required to recite the Ten Commandments before taking the test didn't tend to cheat. Similar studies using agreements to not cheat worked as well. The mere reminder of a moral code changed the outcomes significantly every time.

Our tendency to drift into fudging a test a little is no different than everyday life choices from skipping that workout to being rude to someone around us. We have to constantly remind ourselves about a code that we want to live by. It's the reason the Girl and Boy Scouts have Scout's Law and the military has core values like "Honor, Courage and Commitment". These are there to be a reminder of a standard they want the members to hold themselves to.

This is the essence of character baselines; they are the baseline, a minimum standard we hold ourselves to. The only difference is that character baselines are tailored for ourselves. They are what we truly want for ourselves, not necessarily morals but our own personal code that helps drive everything we do. What is it that is most important for us to live by, to be reminded of day in and day out?

Too Much, Too Perfect

The fact that we have religion and various groups providing morals and values like have integrity and such is fine and dandy. But for some reason, many of us aren't living completely by these teachings, even if we are a member of these groups. There's limited evidence suggesting one way or another but there's a good chance at least part of the reason is because it's either too much or too perfect. We can't live by a code that says don't have sex when we want to have sex. We can't live by a code saying be obedient when we don't agree with whatever it is someone is trying to get us to do.

Morals and right or wrong aside, the point is that often, we are going to break rules and codes that are too much or too perfect. Since that's the case, why not build some rules for things we can agree to? Why not find things that we really do want to live by that we can actually hold ourselves to, not because we feel required to or pressured to but because we genuinely want to?

Take Action

Having a personal code may seem trivial but don't forget the study on the cheating students. All it takes is a reminder and we act differently than we would without the reminder. Create baselines that are meaningful to you and you alone and remind yourself every day. Keep them in your purse or wallet, on your computer background, on your desk, or wherever you need to remember and live by them. They will make it easier to navigate life, giving our precious willpower a break. So, the next time you have eight seconds to make a choice, whether it's to cheat on a test, help someone on the side of the road, or eat ice cream, make sure you follow your own code.

Selfish, Consistent and Keeping our Word

You're five years old and you've been told that "Tomorrow we're going to do your favorite activity! How does that sound?" You feel ecstatic. "Yaaaaaay!!! Wooohoooo!" You can't wait until the next day. You tell everyone what you're going to do. When you go to bed, you can barely sleep because you're thinking about all the cool stuff you'll be doing. If your parents told you the next day, "We're really sorry but there's been a change of plans. We can't go today," imagine how we'd feel as a kid; we'd be upset and confused "But you promised!" Why do some kids react stronger than others and what if the same thing that affected us as children continues to affect us as adults?

Reasonably Unreasonable

While on one hand, as a parent or bystander, we would probably think, "Please get over it, kid. It's not a big deal." And it's true; it's not a big deal in the grand scheme of things. Those shifty emotions are always so difficult to manage for adults, let alone a child.

When something good is about to happen, the brain releases

chemicals for good things coming: happiness and excitement. When something bad is about to happen, similarly, chemicals are released to prepare us for those bad things. Imagine getting a shot of adrenaline and a dose of sleeping pills at the same time. Our body ends up fighting itself to regulate and normalize; being unable to sleep and extremely tired at the same time is not a good feeling. There could be a similar process occurring when we are feeling conflicting or underdeveloped emotions.

We may be acting unreasonable but it's completely understandable for a kid to feel this way, given the situation. The question is, how would we help the child learn to cope with these disconnected feelings, the sense of being let down? Just giving things time is always a fallback but there is something more we can do for the child to help them learn to regulate their emotions.

Pets and Consistency

For those who have pets and have trained them, one thing that may be noticed is that whatever it is we want our pets to do, we need to be very consistent so the pet can learn the pattern. For example, if we want the dog to go to the bathroom outside, we need to be consistent in how we give the dog times to go outside. Eventually, as the dog learns what to do, we can start to relax on the consistent times but be consistent about letting the dog out when the dog is wanting to be let out. If we aren't consistent, the dog won't understand anything about what he or she should or shouldn't be doing and won't learn to trust what we will or won't do at any given time. How will the dog know that he should wait to go to the bathroom if he can't trust that we'll let him out in time?

Not to compare a kid to a pet but there are many similarities with respect to being consistent. If a parent randomly disciplines their child for not doing homework but doesn't do so consistently, what are they teaching the child? A consistent parent that is consistently deficient could arguably be better for a child than a parent that is randomly deficient. With the randomly deficient parent, the child has no idea what they are going to get any given day, leading to higher anxiety.

As a possible analogy, there are studies with rats that may shed light on this phenomenon. When rats are administered consistent shocks versus random shocks, both bad occurrences, the ones exposed to random shocks demonstrated much more overall fear and helplessness than the rats that were administered consistent shocks. What this amounts to is a predictable threat versus an unpredictable threat. When things are completely unpredictable and negative, it amounts to ultimately more chronic stress and helplessness.

This doesn't mean we have to be consistent all the time. This is only to emphasize that consistency *at the right times* is crucial in training and development. After a time, consistency can and probably should taper off as the child (or pet) learns to navigate to the beat of their own drum and to handle more scenarios. If we've been consistent at the right points, the pet will do its best to hold its bladder when we're running late and the child won't throw a fit when we tell them sorry, we can't do that fun thing today.

Internal Consistency

If we move from pets and children to ourselves, we'll find that consistency matters in our own cases too. Remember that our bodies and minds have involuntary aspects to them; what we choose to do consistently is going to govern how those involuntary aspects react to situations. We can train our bodies and minds to do a lot of things and that training is done through some form of consistent work or effort toward something.

We build habits through this internal consistency. We build a lot of what we do and achieve on top of the foundation of consistent habits and actions. If we get good grades, it's because we consistently put in the work. If we are good athletes, it's because we are consistently playing or training in that sport. The compound effect of building habits and constantly growing is a result of some form of internal consistency about tackling a goal or task.

Keeping Our Word

It goes without saying that we should keep our word in day-to-day situations. Why exactly, though? Because it's a lie and lies are bad? We don't think of not keeping our word as lying when it's something simple like promising a child we'll go to the park. There was no intention of lying; life just happened.

We can't go to the extreme and never make a promise, or never make any statements like, "I'll be there." But we also can't keep saying we'll be there when we never make it. The thing is, this isn't necessarily for the person we are making promises to. It isn't about lying or not. If we miss the park, that is pretty insignificant compared to not paying our bills because we chose the park over work. Our friend, our kid, or loved one will get over it, assuming it's not a common theme.

Keeping our word isn't so we can stay on people's good sides; it's all about the effect it has on our mindsets. If we are consistently making promises and not keeping them, we're also making the habit of breaking promises. When a promise is consistently broken, what can we tell ourselves when it's time to really do something?

We won't even be able to say, "I'm going to work out tomorrow," or "I'm going to make sure to get it done today" or make any commitment "in sickness and in health." Consistently breaking our promises is telling ourselves that it's ok, that any and everything we say or promise isn't really that serious. We can just drift and do whatever we want, whenever we want.

That sounds like a great thing, but it would be like rolling dice. It may be a great ride for a while but the moment we really need to get something done, help someone, or do something for ourselves, we'd lack the discipline to hold ourselves to it. If we truly want to do whatever we want, whenever we want, we shouldn't make promises we can't keep.

Consistently Inconsistent

What if we want to be consistent but life is throwing all types of obstacles at us? How do we stay consistent when we barely know what will happen tomorrow or the next day? Being consistent isn't a matter of taking the exact same action every day as much as it's about handling and managing the situations being thrown at us in a consistent way.

If, for example, we know we have inconsistent priorities occurring every day in our lives, it would not be rational to promise to do something the next day unless we made it the true priority. It means we would handle inconsistencies consistently. We'd have a mechanism in place to prioritize things as possible. Instead of making promises that we can't keep, we simply wouldn't make those promises unless we made it a true priority. For everyone's sanity, being consistent and saying, "Sorry, I can't commit to that but I'll try to make it" every time is much better than saying, "Of course, I'll definitely be there."

To Be or Not to Be ... Selfish

Let's say we're a doctor who's always on call. Anytime the phone rings when we're home, there's an emergency that we're needed for. It doesn't help that we already work long hours. Imagine getting an emergency call and having to say, "Sorry, I can't save that person's life right now. I made a promise to hang out with my kid."

It's simply not fair but the example is to underscore an extreme situation and make the case that even a doctor needs to be selfish to take care of themselves. They need their own family time, their own self-care time. Even if someone may die if they aren't there, it simply isn't possible to put all the responsibility on them to be able to help 24/7. There have to be boundaries in place and it's up to us to make sure those boundaries are reasonable for ourselves.

This translates to many areas of life. We simply have to be selfish to an extent and take care of ourselves before we can take care of others. If we aren't in good health, how are we going to take care of someone else's health? If we don't have money, how are we going to help someone with resources? If we don't have our own mental and emotional strength, how are we going to be a shoulder to lean on? We need to selfishly ensure we are taking care of ourselves before we help others.

Selfishly Caring

All in all, we should work on being consistent and keeping our word. It will help those we interact with and, ultimately, ourselves. The importance of consistency and keeping our word cannot be stressed enough. The difference between uncontrollable emotions and controllable ones, the difference between instant gratification and delayed gratification, the difference between sticking to a goal and giving up, the difference between achieving our goals and not achieving them all starts with consistency and keeping our word. And to do that, we have to be selfish about making sure we take care of ourselves.

For those still not sold on the idea of being selfish or taking it to the extreme, think about it this way: while being selfish seems to be a dichotomy to caring for others, it's not optimal to have one without the other. When we help others, we ultimately get more benefit than if we just cared about ourselves. It is to our advantage to help others. And not only that, when we help ourselves, we are making choices, learning, growing and working to achieve things. Ultimately, those achievements will have an impact or be impacted by others. We can't get around interacting with and impacting others even if we wanted to, so why not just accept it? Take advantage of it and be selfishly, consistently committed to caring.

INTERPERSONAL

"The best way to find yourself is to lose yourself in the service of others" -Mahatma Gandhi

Being Misunderstood
by the Brick Wall

You're talking to someone about a charged subject, something that gets the emotions going, something that is important to you. You express your point of view and they disagree, seem to ignore your points and continue to express their own points. Trying your best to get through, you attempt to address each of the points they make and offer your counter-argument. Again, they seem to ignore all of your counter-arguments and express that you are wrong and give other ideas they believe about the subject. You go back and forth in this same manner a couple of times and you start to get frustrated. You feel like you are talking to a brick wall. Are you frustrated because they disagree? Or are you frustrated because they aren't understanding or trying to understand your points?

When One Plus One Doesn't Equal Two

I'm sure many people just want to be right. If we make a choice, if we have an opinion, of course, we made that choice and hold that opinion because we think (or know) it's right. If we acknowledge other people's opinions, doesn't that mean we are wrong or could be wrong? How are we supposed to acknowledge or understand someone who doesn't agree that

1 + 1 = 2?

In the ideal world, we would acknowledge there are always assumptions we have relating to our opinion. Even something as simple as 1 + 1 = 2. This has many assumptions. We are assuming that "1" is the number one, "2" is the number two and that the + sign means to add, etc. This sounds redundant but it's massively crucial: 1 + 1 literally doesn't always equal 2.

Given a different context and different assumptions, we come to different conclusions. The fact is, everything down to the way we add is subject to assumptions, so ideally, we *always* acknowledge other opinions because of the infinite number of assumptions. These assumptions will always cause variations in opinions.

Seek to Understand

When we accept that we aren't right about all of our opinions, we can instead seek to understand other possibilities when we communicate with others. Based on our understanding and experiences, we can trust we've made the best choice for ourselves but know there are always other possibilities that others may lean toward.

By working to understand other's opinions, they see a genuine attempt to get to know their side. They will often be more willing to get to know our opinions as a result. It not only helps to strengthen our own knowledge but helps them understand a different possible outcome:

```
1 + 1 = 2   (our assumed outcome)

1 + 1 = 10  (binary addition)

1 + 1 = 11  (concatenation)
```

Whoever we are talking to may stick to 1 + 1 = 10 as a key assumption. Every opinion is then formed around that assumption and as such, they will have different conclusions about many things. If they understand our assumptions and we understand theirs, we can now speak the same language, make decisions better and have useful and possibly fun discussions.

Facts Are Facts

The problem is, of course, when we believe or know something is fact and not just an opinion. This closes the door to any alternatives; it establishes that we are making no assumptions.

In math and science, facts are supposed to be the most basic things that can be observed to be true. They should be simple, repeatable, verifiable by everyone. These act as the basis of scientific theory and laws. The beauty of math and science is that they accept that theory and laws all can change, as can the actual facts and their proven observation.

In general, the litmus test for "what is a fact" is whether it is verifiable by everyone. We have to be aware that the vast majority of our beliefs are not facts; they are opinions. For example, historical facts are not scientific facts. They can't be repeated or measured to verify. We only have books and records that one has to believe are true.

Statistical evidence also is often used to make factual claims, which are subject to many assumptions. We may think statistics equals "repeatable and measurable by everyone" and, therefore, "fact." But unfortunately, it depends on what we are measuring and what we are concluding. Statistical evidence may have strong implications; it may be used as the basis for decisions, but it is not typically a fact and always comes with certain assumptions.

We must be diligent and true to ourselves, acknowledging when, despite our strongest beliefs, if it is not repeatable, measurable and verifiable by everyone, it's not a fact.

When We Hit a Brick Wall

Now, despite all of our efforts, we will encounter brick walls that believe that all of their assumptions and opinions are facts. They will not acknowledge any of our points or counter-arguments, even if we acknowledge and understand theirs.

These brick walls could be our own parents or family members, our spouse or significant other, or our friends. In most cases, there's no reason to push the envelope. It may suck or hurt that they don't understand or acknowledge anything we are saying. Yet, it is almost never a good idea to force the issue. If we hit the brick wall and break it down, we hurt the other person and if it's someone we care about, we hurt ourselves as well.

As much as I wish there was a trick to help everyone become more understanding of differing opinions, all we can do is be as reasonable as possible when we hit a brick wall, be open to their opinions, acknowledge the differences and spread the message by being an example. Give them something to soften their wall, then go around the wall and leave them be. Hopefully we can slowly improve one person at a time.

Jerks and Pushovers

You're walking up to the convenience store and as you are heading in, another customer is also walking up, maybe two steps ahead of you. They proceed to open the door and as you reach to grab the handle, you realize they didn't wait or attempt to hold it for you and it swiftly shut behind them in your face.

In some areas, no one would think twice about it; they'd open the door and keep on going. In other areas, the person in front would be viewed as a jerk since they didn't hold the door. And sometimes, you who had the door shut in your face would get laughed at — perfect for a meme.

Perfect World

No one wants to be a pushover, but plenty accept being a jerk. There's actually logic to it. If everyone were pushovers, then things would work just fine. No one would step on another and everyone would hold doors for others. If no one took advantage and everyone was nice and looked after each other, this would be the most ideal way of living. In this type of society, there wouldn't be a pushover because no one would be pushing anyone else over. They'd just be happy functioning members of society, nice people.

A single jerk in this perfect world, however, would pretty much rule. The unfortunate truth is that we not only have a single jerk; we have a ton of them. We live in a world where people will deliberately try to get over on others and push them over to get their own way. This ranges from the most insignificant actions, like spending a moment to hold a door, to more extreme situations, like theft or violence. A pushover in this environment can get steamrolled.

Nice People

It's sad because, most likely, the pushover was raised in a good home; their family taught them good values and to care for all things. They taught them not to fight, to be a bigger person. They are pretty much a nice person.

Nice people, however, are often seen as soft targets for theft, panhandlers and anyone else seeking to take advantage of others. So-called friends will leech off of nice people if they have money. Partners or significant others will have them at their beck and call. If they are driving in New York traffic, they will never make it out without cutting someone off, which they've been taught not to do. Their extreme consideration for others could carry into everything under the sun, resulting in everyone else appearing to walk over them constantly. The issue isn't that everyone else is being a jerk; it may be that the nice person isn't asserting themselves. No one knows what the overly nice person actually wants or needs.

Jerk Code

Interestingly enough, there's somewhat of a "jerk code." The jerk that doesn't think twice to push someone else over will eventually have to watch themselves. They will encounter other jerks and have to fight it out in some form all the time.

If they are in business, they could lose their money because they won't form a healthy network of relationships. Since business and life both need others to be successful, being a jerk all the time isn't a viable solution.

The same way our perfect world didn't work with one single jerk, having nothing but jerks would also not work because they'd essentially destroy each other. Jerks would have to be nice sometimes.

Perspective and Context

One of our biggest themes seems to always surround context and perspective. We must constantly remember that everything we witness or observe is through our own perspective. We have to be aware that we may not understand the full context of any particular situation.

For example, in our door-holding scenario, maybe the person in front of us was completely unaware of us being right behind them. It is often the case that what we consider being a jerk is simply our own perspective. It's like the woman who is considered a bitch for not smiling and turning away an interested man.

There are so many unfortunate misunderstandings that it is often more efficient to assume the person is not a jerk while, at the same time, always protecting ourselves.

Inner Jerk and Pushover

To the jerks of the world, you're also a pushover. You live in a world where someone with more power than you can and will push you over if they get the chance. The jerk with more power could be anyone from a thug on the street with a gun to whoever writes your paycheck. You wouldn't appreciate that, right? You'd fight it, right? Then, it's up to you to not push others over wrongly and be a decent person. Refusing to be pushed over doesn't mean you become a jerk to everyone else before they have a chance. Being cautious is ok but being a jerk to everyone will ultimately result in getting burnt.

To the pushovers or nice people of the world, we all have an inner jerk — embrace it. It needs to be let free sometimes, not to everyone but when a jerk is about to push you over, summon your inner jerk and don't let them push you down. Learn to say NO. Establish boundaries that are reasonable and meaningful and push back if necessary.

P.S.

Becoming a jerk because someone didn't hold the door isn't a good reason. Neither is being cut off in traffic. If you notice your boundaries or reasons to be a jerk are retaliatory in nature or to show another jerk the error in their ways, those are not good reasons and you may be an actual jerk. Having your own sense of justice is great but forcing others to acknowledge or live by them, not so much.

Crappy Co-Workers

You're excited. It's your first day on the new job. You got a decent raise and are new to the area. You have a little bit of experience with this type of job, so it's not completely foreign to you. Everyone you meet has been friendly and the workload doesn't seem to be unreasonable. You're assigned to work with another person and both of you all will be on the same team doing the same job but your co-worker is in more of the lead role since they've been there longer.

Fast forward a month and your dream job has turned into a nightmare. The job isn't getting done well. The supervisor is on you to do better, be faster. Your co-worker, who is still always nice to you, seems to have been giving you misleading tasks and guidance. You can't figure out if it's on purpose, by mistake, or if you're just not understanding something. Your supervisor is questioning your abilities and you're hearing rumors that another co-worker has been talking about how you need more training. There's the legitimate threat of losing your job.

Crappy Co-Worker Types

There's no such thing as an official list of crappy co-worker types but the common theme typically is selfish gain or not doing their job in some way. Here are some types many of us may resonate with:

Middle manager syndrome. This person may or may not be in a lead role but they want to be the manager, lead, or get promoted so badly that they will do whatever it takes, throw anyone under the bus, as long as it serves their purpose of looking good so they can get a promotion. They steal credit whenever possible. We need to be aware of their tactics.

Warm bodies. They make excuses or find ways to not do any real work. That means they know the system and know how to work it to their benefit. These types are dangerous for anyone trying to get work done because they know so much about how to avoid work that they can twist things, whisper to just the right people, convince others that the overachiever is doing more harm than good. Warm bodies want to keep their easy spot just the way it is, so anyone impacting that should be aware.

No backbone. Co-workers with no-backbone are usually in a lead, supervisor, or management role. They are usually nice, listen to concerns and may have good ideas. They aren't always easy to spot because, when things are going well, they will be great co-workers. However, when conflict arises, they won't bat for the team and they avoid conflict like the plague. If there's a personnel problem, they won't hold them accountable because they won't be willing to have that direct conversation. This means their team will have no real support when they need it most.

Gossiping co-workers. They may or may not have bad intentions but talks about others so much that there's always something negative coming up about someone. They gossip excessively and they also don't take into consideration anyone's feelings or any predicament they may put someone in by talking about them.

Rice-bowlers. They are usually a subject matter expert in some form. They know everything about their job but they don't share that knowledge, usually, because they don't have time to train others. They position themselves to be the only person to do the work either intentionally or because they have zero faith that anyone else can do the work. These co-workers can leave a major gap when they quit and if we're on their team, we'll be stuck holding the bag.

Haters and extremists. They are anything from jealous, to racist, to chauvinistic, to whatever hate-filled or misguided soup they partake in. While, on one hand, they could be the most difficult to deal with because they are driven by likely deep-rooted issues; they also could be the easiest to deal with. They may not do much of anything. They either give nasty looks or fall into one of the other categories. Being really good at the job and staying modest usually quiets these types up.

Damage Control

Before anything, if we're in a negative work situation dealing with crappy co-workers, we need to cover our butts and do damage control. All this means is that we limit the reasons anyone can have a problem with us. In other words, those extended lunches, coming in late, leaving early, missing meetings, or being on the phone or on Facebook too much is not an option.

This also means that if we communicate, we take into consideration who is or could be listening and we ensure we mind our business and handle our business. Make sure there are others around when taking tasking and whenever possible, copy all parties on emails and always follow up with something written if taking verbal tasks over the phone, in person, or in meetings.

Depending on the type of crappy co-worker, we will need to make sure they have as little ammo to use against us as possible.

Accept Responsibility

When our job sucks because of co-workers that are talking negatively about us or are somehow negatively impacting our performance, it can be extremely annoying. So, we have to try not to do things in the heat of our emotions. Once we've taken a breather and calmed down by acknowledging our emotions, we can figure out the causes. Before that, however, we have to have an open mind to the whole situation, and we have to accept responsibility.

We have a role in every situation we are in; for example, a coach accepts responsibility for the team despite individual team members' problems. In our scenario, accepting responsibility may be insanely difficult because it seems to be clearly the co-worker's fault. That may be the case but by accepting responsibility, we are accepting that there are things within our ability to change. If we cannot do that, we will not only fail but we will not be able to grow from the failure. This is massively important and is a recurring theme in every failure situation.

For example, a bus driver who crashes due to a brake failure accepted the responsibility of driving others despite any possible risks or outcomes. That means that even if it wasn't truly their fault, they still need to learn everything possible about the situation, so if there's a way for them to prevent an accident in the future, they will do so.

Be Better than Everyone at the Job

Before we even think about trying to solve the problem, we need to make sure we are the best. If we are new, then we may need to stay late and study after work. This is another extremely difficult thing to do and accept. Often, we will want to use being new as a reason for not being able to be as well as our co-workers.

Most people don't want to do more than everyone else in normal work circumstances. But if we're in a negative predicament, there isn't any real choice. The thing is, most likely, if we worked better, harder and longer than the rest, the vast majority of problems at work would disappear. So, this concept must always be practiced and improved upon.

Introspect and Strategize

Once we truly have accepted responsibility and we've started the path of being the best we can be at the job, we can then start to understand possible causes of the current situation. What role did we play? What about our indirect contributions or areas that we may not have realized we are doing because we don't fully understand all the moving parts?

If there are areas that we don't fully understand or training that we need, we have to acknowledge that. We have to then come up with goals or targets to attack and figure out ways to accomplish them, so we don't get put in the same situation in the future.

That means we need to think multiple steps ahead. We need to have an idea of how our co-workers and our supervisor will respond and how things will be perceived. Know their best-case reactions and their worst-case reactions. Having an idea of their style of crappiness can work wonders.

One on One

Once we have a way forward, even if it doesn't involve our co-worker, if they truly instigated or have a hand in this problem, they need to be addressed one on one. Many of us will want to skip this step if there's a way to move forward without addressing the co-worker directly. That may save face or cause the least conflict in the short-term but it's the same as avoiding a bully by going around the school, or worse yet, just telling the teacher without telling the bully first. The problem could easily come back to haunt us.

We have to literally address them, talk to them truthfully and ideally as transparently as possible. The problem is, while this is the rational and proper answer, this can also put us in a potentially more vulnerable position.

That's why we have to have plans in place. We have to know the vulnerabilities and how to address them based on the worst-case scenarios. This one-on-one talk is about respect as well as our way of acknowledging that we may be missing something glaring, just in case there are things we don't fully know about the co-worker or the situation.

All Together Now

If we've done all the other steps and still are encountering problems, we need to have a get-together. All the major players in the problem need to be invited into the same room — that means the supervisor and our crappy co-worker at a minimum.

In many cases, the reason things aren't getting fixed is everyone is on a different page. Notice we aren't advocating to speak with the supervisor alone first. This is because any good supervisor or leader taking two different team member's perspectives shouldn't arbitrarily trust one over another. There is no way to ensure shared perspectives aside from having everyone in the room at the same time.

Give It Time, Then Get Out

If we've done all this, we have to remember a city isn't built in a day. We have to give it time, show everyone we aren't going anywhere and we're going to make things better, whether they like it or not. The general rule is to give any job a year. Not only do most employers not like to see short-term employment but it also ensures we've given it our all and committed to trying to make things work. The more extreme the situation, the sooner we can pull out the parachute.

This, of course, is only a guideline; there is no always right answer. If we've truly given it our all and a reasonable amount of time and it still doesn't feel right, get out ASAP.

For Everyone

We all have some crappiness in us. Usually, it's when we aren't doing what we want to do or have other issues in our life. Ever have to do a project that makes no sense or that adds no value? What about doing work that is supposed to be someone else's job? How about doing tasks that we can teach a monkey to do and is completely soul-sucking? What if we are getting paid less than everyone else by an extreme margin to do the same job? What if we have an extremely negative home situation?

We can all easily become the crappy co-worker who we get

annoyed with when we are encountering less than ideal situations. Since we all have the potential to be crappy, we have to accept it and not be so hard on our co-workers. Acknowledge the potential inner crappiness and do better, not just for everyone else but for ourselves.

The same way emotions can speak volumes about what we want, our inner crappiness can too. Whenever we aren't doing a good job, whenever we are consistently impacting others negatively, there's a good chance there's more to it. If we don't want to be there, find a way to be somewhere else through hard work, perseverance, and, of course, good ol' failure.

Taken Advantage of
(Or Ripped Off)

You take something expensive to a repair shop; they give you a price and tell you to come back in three months. You hear they are the best to do what they do, so you figure it's worth the wait. They require a 30% down payment to start the work as a good faith payment. Fast forward three months and they aren't done yet. Fast forward another month and they aren't done yet. When you finally approach them firmly to say you need everything back, they show you that it's in pieces and is not done yet. They say they can give you back the pieces, but they will have to keep your 30%.

As is expected, your anger goes through the roof but since you've read about managing anger, you calm yourself down to figure out the right decision first. You tell them that if they can't give you everything back or the monetary value, you'll have to pursue further action. They say go ahead, that they have no money or assets. Friends tell you that you have to be firm and keep going back to them, that if it were them, they'd be able to make them do what they are supposed to do.

The Advantage

When we are taken advantage of, our first thoughts are often to somehow get back at the person and get back whatever it is they took from us. The thing is that *is* the advantage—when someone takes advantage of us, they have the upper hand. We've given them something, given them the advantage. In our scenario, we gave the advantage with the supposed promise of something in return.

It could be outright fraud or theft to an extent but if we think about it, this happens everywhere, from businesses to pan-handlers, to salespeople, to relationships. We're all negotiating to try and get whatever we want out of the interaction. This may sound cold, but of course, it's not; it can be full of feelings, both good and bad.

In relationships, for example, someone could want our money, our body and our time and give little to nothing in return, selling us on the promise of something eventually in the future.

The Exchange

The thing is, we live in a world where we have to sometimes ensure that we have the advantage and not the other way around. It all depends on what is at stake and what risk we are willing to take. If we think of it as a business transaction, both sides want to get the most advantage as possible. In a more personal environment, both sides just don't want to be screwed over.

In either case, however, it's up to us to manage what it is we give and expect in return. Would we, for example, give a random stranger off the street a large sum of money and something we own of value and tell them to give it back to us in three months?

Of course, we wouldn't do that; then why are we going to trust a random repair shop? We may not normally think of this in terms or risks, but we are taking risks every time we give away our advantage.

Even Terms

The most ideal situation is that the terms are somewhat even. If we have to give something, they have to give us something in return. Many business transactions are this way—a service gets performed and money gets rendered in exchange. That way, the business performing the service can withhold their results/work and the client getting the service isn't paying until the service is provided.

Even relationships should be operating on some form of even terms, some form of mutual satisfaction. The problem with relationships is that the terms are intangible; they can never really be measured. Also, with relationships, there's affection that doesn't really apply or work when constantly trying to balance out terms. However, no matter the situation, communicating before any sort of exchange is important. This goes for all significant transactions, business or personal.

Trust but Verify

There comes a time when even terms aren't possible for some reason. In business, typically, that means there's some form of leverage. They have what we want so badly that we're willing to take a risk and give them the advantage. Ideally, this is when some form of insurance comes into play so we can let the insurance companies do the dirty work.

Unfortunately, in more personal situations, there isn't any insurance for crappy encounters. So instead, we have to verify a bit before we make an exchange. We have to understand more about the service or person we're dealing with. Otherwise, we have to treat them no differently than a random stranger off the street.

If we wouldn't give a random stranger money to hold, then we shouldn't give money to a random business owner who we know nothing about either. Having a business definitely doesn't make someone more trustworthy; in fact, some could argue it's the opposite. The bottom line is, even in a relationship, we need to have a decent idea of who we are dealing with if we are willing to give them the advantage and take that risk.

The Responsibility

This final concept is polarizing and that is, we have to take responsibility for being ripped off or taken advantage of. It doesn't mean the other person wasn't in the wrong. It means that we *knowingly* gave someone else the advantage by entrusting money, time, or whatever else to them. This is a hard pill to swallow.

This doesn't infer we shouldn't trust others; just that when we trust others, we have to acknowledge the risk of getting screwed over. And when we get screwed over, we have to acknowledge that was part of the deal. That's why it was a risk in the first place. If we were able to always get everything back, it wouldn't be a risk, and no one would ever have the advantage.

It's ok to try to get things back and even things up. We just need to acknowledge that getting even and trying to retrieve something we've lost to an advantage won't often go well.

Imagine a situation where someone betrayed our trust in a non-monetary way. It's like a cracked egg. No matter how hard we try, we can never get the egg back to the way it was originally. It's not usually worthwhile to chase getting even because often times it simply isn't possible.

Being taken advantage of sucks, so ideally, we must ensure that every exchange is mutually beneficial at all times to some extent. If there are reasons that we want to allow someone to have the advantage, that's definitely ok; as long as we're doing it because the risk, situation or person is worth it no matter what happens.

Dating: Keeping It Real vs. Being Nice

You've had about four or five dates over the course of a month with someone you're interested in. The person you've been seeing is nice, cool, attractive and pretty much your type. They indicated they are looking for a relationship and things seem to have been progressing normally. Now, however, Friday is here and for the last several weeks, the two of you have coordinated something to do before the weekend hit. So, you text them to see if they are doing anything and ask if they'd like to check out a new spot. They decline with no explanation. "Not a big deal," you think but something about the interaction was awkward, not like the rest of your interactions. You let it go and randomly chat like you used to, but they aren't responding much anymore. They take a day or more to respond and when they do, it's not engaging at all. By the second week of no dates, you figure they are moving on.

Even though you get the gist, sometimes it's nice to get a clear answer, especially if it's someone you're interested in. At least, that's what you think, so you point out the elephant and ask if something changed or if they just aren't interested anymore. They respond with an equally direct response: "Do you want the truth?"

Keeping It Real

When confronted with a question like, "Do you want the truth?", it's a somewhat unfair question. Of course, you can say, "No, thanks. Keep it to yourself." But something about the question makes it feel like there's only one answer: "Yes, of course, I want the truth." Then, when this person proceeds to tell you, "Ok, some people say they want the truth but don't actually mean it" … brace yourself because they will likely proceed to tell you a series of things that judge you, some of which you may already feel self-conscious about. "Well, you are out of shape and overweight, talk too much and ramble, don't initiate physical contact enough and have a really big nose."

"Wow," you think to yourself. You don't even know how to respond. In fact, you don't respond. What are you supposed to do with that "truth"? "They can take that truth and…." Now that you are thinking about it, why did you want the truth anyway? Because you were curious? Because maybe you'd think about trying to be a better person? Because maybe there was a chance?

Being Nice

Imagine, instead of asking if you want the truth, they say that they aren't looking for a relationship right now, or they're too busy, or better yet, "It's not you; it's me." These nice answers, if taken seriously, could make you think, "Oh, that's fine, I'm really busy too," as if you could possibly date when things slow down or when they get themselves together. That's not what they mean, of course. They were just trying to be nice, trying to let you down easy and instead, never let you down at all.

It doesn't seem very nice to lead someone on, to allow someone to think there's a chance when there isn't one. Is being nice really for you? No, in many cases, it probably isn't. Most likely, the person trying to be nice is really wanting you to still like them, to still think they are cool, awesome people. So, instead of telling you their thoughts that you'd find issues with, they sugarcoat them but feed you poop.

The Opposing Perspectives

Some would say that keeping it real is important, that you should know why people say things so that you can learn, change, or grow. That is reasonable, yet there is a time and a place for everything. Someone you've dated for a month doesn't have enough in the emotional bank account to make a withdrawal like that. It's the equivalent of listening to an online troll. They may say something that is true, but their context is off, their delivery is off, their point for saying it also is likely off. Being told you talk too much, for example, is not useful to anyone; it is also based on their own limited opinion.

As for being nice, some may feel that not wanting to hurt someone's feelings is truly for the sake of the other person, that it's important to shield them from unnecessary pain. Yet, that's similar to saying that you should catch a child before they fall every time. That's not nice, that's debilitating. Catching a child when they fall every time is bound to create some issues of dependence and reliance. They won't learn to catch themselves. There may be a time and a place but it's rare; and as with the keeping it real example, dating for a month is not one of them.

Self-Confidence, Then Self-Awareness

For those with weak self-confidence, strengthen it. People will think you are unattractive. There will be people who don't like the way you talk, walk, or do anything for that matter. If you cannot accept that fact, build your self-confidence before dating *anyone*. There is no reason to date someone when you haven't established yourself. Self-confidence is being ok with being wrong, unattractive and not wanted because you are ok with yourself.

Once your self-confidence is solid, you need to build your self-awareness. This is understanding what you are capable of and how that relates to everyone else. If you are overweight compared to everyone else, or don't look like a model, or can't play basketball, being aware is important to navigate life. You will know what you do or don't want to focus on, change, improve upon, or leave alone. Also, since you built your self-confidence first, you are ok with yourself and are changing to achieve goals that are meaningful to you, not goals that are rife with confidence problems and other people's opinions.

If you find yourself constantly worrying about other's opinions, stop. Build your self-confidence. If you find yourself constantly dating people who don't like or want you, stop. Build your self-awareness. Rinse, repeat.

Fighting Over the Little Things

Most of us, no matter how cool, calm and collected, have gotten into an argument over something seemingly small. A light was left on, a plate was left in the sink, trash wasn't dumped, a curse word was said, a question wasn't answered, a wrong turn was made, the phone wasn't picked up, we didn't come home in time and on and on. There is an infinite number of little reasons to get into an argument. Despite our knowing that we shouldn't sweat the small stuff, we just can't seem to let go of some things. Maybe we don't care but someone else does? More importantly, is it really just a little thing'?

What Are Little Things Really?

Little things are topics that, on their own, typically have no real significance for most people. A light being left on could be considered a little thing. On its own, without any other context, there isn't a good reason to argue over it. A single plate in the sink with no other context is pretty much irrelevant. No one cares or should care. No arguments or fights should arise if there's no other related information pertaining to the plate in the sink.

When advice is given to not sweat the small things and let go, often they are considering these little things as having no context of importance. This is somewhat of a dilemma; clearly, if we are fighting about it, someone thinks something about the subject is important.

Little Things With Context

Nothing in this world is without context. The plate in the sink got there somehow and it could relate to other things in ways we can't even imagine. To someone, the plate relates to not listening; to another, it translates to a lack of consideration and to yet another, the plate could be unintended evidence.

Many of us have heard the story about the man on the subway with three extremely rowdy, small children. Everyone is looking at the kids and him wondering why he doesn't do something about the kids. When the storyteller says to him, "Sir, your children are disturbing a lot of people," the man looks up as if coming out of a daze and says, "Oh, you're right. We just came from the hospital where their mother died an hour ago. I guess they don't know how to handle it either." (This story is from Stephen Covey in *The 7 Habits of Highly Effective People*).

For the man in the subway, the rowdy kids were insignificant compared to the loss of his wife and their mother. While this is enlightening and helps us keep other little things in perspective, it doesn't help when we know whoever we are arguing with isn't in that type of situation.

We Don't Argue Over Little Things

Contrary to popular belief, we don't argue about little things. We argue about things we believe are important for some reason or another. It's the representation by little things that gets us confused. Since when should having a shoe stepped on result in a fight? Yet to them, that represented some sort of respect that wasn't being given, some sort of acknowledgment or awareness, or a really expensive pair of shoes...

If we or someone else is annoyed or upset about something seemingly small, it's *guaranteed* that something of importance is behind it. If we aren't able to sniff out what the importance is, it also may not be due to one person or event but an aggregation of things.

Often the bigger things being represented are a result of internal conflicts, not simply conflict between others. Internal struggles like this will not only be difficult to detect but even more difficult to resolve.

Social Complexity

One of the biggest problems is that our social interactions are extremely complex. A drill sergeant yelling and barking orders makes sense in a military environment, yet that same drill sergeant working for Google may not do so well if they don't adapt. Every individual, every family, every group, every society, every culture has slightly different ways of interacting with others. Someone that grew up in a family with no yelling may get into bad arguments with someone who starts to raise their voice more quickly. Someone that grew up with a very emotionally expressive family may often fight with someone who grew up in a more emotionless family. The person who places high importance on social praise and respect may react completely differently in public settings.

The point we are driving home is that, between social complexity and the context of the little things, we create a massively complex web of possibilities. We should slow things down the moment someone starts to get heated if not for any

---

other reason than we might not understand their context fully and the complexity surrounding it.

How to Argue Over Important Things

Instead of preaching to not sweat the small stuff, we know it's ok to have disagreements and discuss those disagreements to try to come to some sort of solution to the issue, no matter how small things may seem. We just need to remember a few key things:

1. Understand the context of the little thing. If it seems insignificant, we likely don't understand the context.

2. Acknowledge, agree or compromise. Acknowledging the problem that is being presented is often simple and can sometimes solve the problem without even agreeing.

3. Help others always. If the person we are arguing with starts to get too emotional, slow things down, or walk away immediately.

4. Self-care. If we are losing control of our own emotions, slow things down, walk away and stay away until we regain control.

5. Address importance via emotions. Trying to disengage when getting too heated may indicate to others that it isn't important. Acknowledge that no matter what the argument, someone feels it is important, try to smooth it out as possible.

When Enough Is Enough

Everyone has their limits. It's much easier to walk away or to let things go with strangers. But when our family or friends we live with have these encounters persistently, it can become very stressful for all involved. Ideally, we come to understand the context of the little things so that we can at least navigate around the problems and help out where we can.

But if we're dealing with someone's own internal issues, we're in a relationship where these arguments are too frequent or feel overwhelmingly stressful, then it may be time to walk away or get outside help. Having a professional facilitate conversations or issues could be all that is needed.

We also may just as easily be the cause of the chronic stress as someone else. Relationships and social interactions are not always easy but as long as we work to use our emotions wisely and remember that arguments over little things are usually over something bigger, we'll find a solution.

Extending a Helping Hand and Getting Burned

Everyone usually highlights how helping others is a great thing. However, what about those times we get burned? Have you ever loaned money and never saw it again? Have you ever referred someone to a job and they did something dumb or quit after only a few weeks? Have you ever helped someone out of a predicament, only to be stuck with all the associated issues? It happens and if we're too "nice," it could happen a lot. People suck. But people can be amazing too. What's a good way to keep a balance?

Small Things

Firstly, let's get the small things out of the way. Opening a door for someone who doesn't say thank you or giving a few dollars to a panhandler who uses it for alcohol isn't getting burned, but it's a similar concept. Clearly, that's no reason to stop opening doors for people. But if it happens a lot, it can become the reason we stop doing things for others—no one seems appreciative. For the panhandlers, maybe it's not that they aren't appreciative but that our help isn't really helping in the way we intended.

These are no revelations but they help underscore the most basic level things we really want (or need) when we help others: 1) to be needed, meaningful or worthwhile and 2) to be appreciated. Really, those combine into one: our helping needs to be or feel worthwhile.

Subjective Meaning and Worth

Is it worthwhile to help a panhandler with a few dollars? Ask this question to 10 people and you'll likely get several different answers. If the panhandler used the money for food, many would say, yes, it's worthwhile. If the panhandler used it for drugs, the vast majority would say no, it's not worthwhile. Then there are those who say even if the panhandler used it for food, that we are enabling them the same way we enable a loved one to be spoiled.

With strangers, it's often not realistic to know whether something is worthwhile or not because there's just no telling. They take the money or help and we don't see them ever again. In this case, we are hoping that it's worthwhile. Some of us are more hopeful and assume that it is meaningful and will help. Others are more skeptical and assume that it isn't worthwhile and don't help unless they're more sure of the outcome.

Neither of these positions is right, but again, it helps build context for the bigger issues. Some of us are more hopeful; others are more skeptical. We can't assume the skeptics are jerks who don't help; they just may not see a positive outcome the way a hopeful person would. Everyone's determination of what is worth it is different and there is no right answer. Just know that if it was worth it before helping, it should be worth it after helping, even if we got burned.

Customs and Tradition

What about when we give something because it's tradition or it's just what we do'? For example, when we visit a friend or family member's house for a holiday or special occasion, many of us will bring food or drinks. It's somewhat customary to do so in the same way it is customary to say thank you or show appreciation for bringing said contributions. Returning the favor is, likewise, a custom of sorts. When someone does something for us, we return the favor to both show our appreciation and even things out.

Yet if we bring two apple pies, only to realize there are four apple pies at the party already, we probably will feel like we should have brought something else because it wasn't as worthwhile. If the host threw away the pies saying we don't need them, we definitely wouldn't feel appreciated. Even with tradition, it is still giving. If we follow tradition and somehow don't feel it is worthwhile, we won't like it.

Love and Helping

Imagine your loved one is in a predicament; they need money to pay for a bill. If they don't get that money soon, all types of problems could arise. If we had enough money, many of us, both hopefuls and skeptics alike, would help out and give money to a loved one so that they could get back on their feet. In some cases, we'd try to help, even if we didn't have enough money. We'd do whatever we could to help them out.

With loved ones, helping is the default; it's always worthwhile. We love them, that's what love is. Isn't it giving without expectation of receiving? While for others, maybe it's more a matter of custom, it's what we do. If we have plenty to give, we could argue that there's no problem. We help them out of the predicament and do so as many times as they need.

Enabling Makes It Our Responsibility

Yet something that is a very common theme when we talk about giving to someone with an addiction is the idea that sometimes giving is doing the opposite of what we think from a psychological perspective. It is no different with giving or helping in general. If we help someone get a job every time they need a job, will they be able to get a job on their own? If we pay for someone's bill every time they have a problem, will they learn from that mistake? Or will they just rely on us when there's a problem?

The somewhat ugly truth is that we may instinctively want to be relied on. If that's the case, then we have to accept the full responsibility of what that entails. If their problems start to weigh on us and we've been enabling them the whole time, drawing the line is unreasonable and not truly helping. It's the same as a parent who enabled their child from 0-25 years old and then wants to kick them out and force them to be on their own. Helping someone can take a long-term effort, similar to the amount of time spent enabling. In fact, it may never change if it has gone on too long, especially without professional help.

Giving Versus Helping

For some of us, giving for the sake of it just feels good. As for simple gifts, there is nothing wrong with that at all; have at it. Yet, when someone has come to rely on our gifts and it becomes a recurring gift that is needed, that has clearly gone into the enabling phase. At that point, we need to be smarter about how we are giving versus how we are helping.

We've used these two terms somewhat similarly because we typically see them interchangeably; yet we want to establish a divide. Giving is more altruistic — providing things without expectation of anything in return. Ideally, these things should be worthwhile to at least some extent. Even the most altruistic gift has a price: it needs to be worthwhile to someone.

Now with helping, on the other hand, we don't help for the sake of helping. We are working to improve *someone else's* situation to the greatest extent within our means. That means although we are helping, it is someone else's responsibility. If we help without providing that person the means to help themselves, we aren't truly helping the person; we're temporarily changing their immediate situation and enabling them to rely on us, which is ultimately hurting them and potentially us as well.

Helping Is Like Coaching

What this means is that when we truly help someone, we are like a coach. We are working with them to become better able to handle their situation. Throwing money over the fence, paying for something isn't helping anyone in the long term without deliberate methods and verification of some sort of result along the way.

A coach can't play the game for the players. A coach can't make the shots for them or take the burden of their training away. A coach has to help a player understand why the training is necessary and explain and teach what is needed to achieve their goals.

So, if we want to help someone by giving money, we have to be a coach. Ask them to do something positive toward the ultimate goals in exchange. Have them work on whatever it is will help them out of their situation permanently. If they don't want to, then it should become clear that their responsibilities and issues go beyond what we should be taking on without professional help.

Other People's Business Is Business

Giving and helping without expectation of things in return doesn't seem to happen. When we do *anything* in relation to others, we are getting into their business, their responsibilities, their situations. If we stick our nose into other people's business, when we give or help, we have to believe that it is worthwhile, that it is of value to the person being helped. Otherwise, what is the point of giving or helping?

Just like in business, sometimes people don't want help the way we gave it. Sometimes people want more than we are willing to give. Sometimes things don't go our way and we get burned for helping. But that's ok as long as we recognize when someone isn't willing to work on helping themselves. We can limit being burned. As long as we are doing our best to provide something worthwhile and to help others help themselves, it should all work out and our burns will be worth it in the end.

P.S. Giving or Taking

It shouldn't need to be said but seriously, if we haven't helped ourselves, we have no business helping others. If we are subtly or unknowingly weighing down our own friends, family, or significant others due to taking on the responsibility of others and helping, are we really giving? Or are we taking?

Growing Apart and Cutting Friendships

You have a friend who's been around for years, through ups and downs. You became friends when you lived nearby, going to school or work but once you moved a couple of hours away, the relationship seemed to slip. Instead of going out or seeing each other every day, it started to become every week. Then after every week, it became every month. And now it's about twice a year. The calls and chats in between also started getting more and more sparse. There's no reason to cut off the friendship just because you don't talk as much but they are getting upset that you don't hang out enough. Is it because of life or because you are simply growing apart?

Friendship Meter

Let's dissect what a friend means first; I know it may seem trivial but bear with me for a second. Friends are defined as sharing some sort of mutual affection; we simply like each other. The degree of friendship, then, depends on the degree that we like each other. For a strong friendship, we could even say we love each other. The main complication is that it has to be *mutual* affection, not one-sided affection or lopsided affection. So, a friendship ends up being as strong as whoever has the lowest amount of affection, the amount that is mutual.

Unfortunately for us, there's no friend affection meter that we can use to determine how much affection we should release. If we release too much, then we look like idiots that love someone who doesn't care and if we release too little, we look like jerks who don't realize someone cares about us. So, we end up constantly monitoring this friendship meter to increase or decrease the love.

Where's the Love

Since we don't have a friendship meter we all can see, we have to figure it out for ourselves. Often the go-to is how much time is spent together. The more time together equates to more love. We don't even think about doing it, but we assume those who are around us the most are those who care the most. However, time together is not the only factor in how much someone loves us.

So, what else is there? One framework by Gary Chapman describes five love languages: gifts, words of affirmation, acts of service, physical touch, and, of course, quality time. This isn't an end-all-be-all list. For example, where is listening or a shoulder to cry on? Are those acts of service? Or silent affirmation? In either case, these love languages at least give a framework that we can use to broaden our perspective outside of focusing on time spent together.

Keeping Score

Once we have a better understanding of how people show their affection, we can start to fill up the friendship meter with more inputs. Maybe we don't spend much time together but the random visit with a small gift or words of encouragement may count for more than multiple get-togethers. What does this score really mean though? Does any amount of scoring give us an understanding of how much someone truly cares?

There may be a scientific way to provide evidence for this, but everyone's scoring would be so different that it would be difficult to track. One person may care immensely about someone else and be the best at listening and be a shoulder to cry on, but they only demonstrate that when there's a problem. Another person may be the type that really likes quality time but is extremely busy and so a chat every few weeks is all they end up doing, despite their love.

And then there's the person who doesn't actually care but read the manual and knows exactly when to give gifts and words of affirmation just to get on someone's good side. That would wreak havoc on any scorekeeping because we'd be fooled or simply wrong about how much someone actually cares.

Tit for Tat

This scorekeeping isn't just in relation to directly showing affection. It's in any giving and taking. For example, separating a bill equally versus paying for the bill versus not offering to pay. These may not have any bearing on how much someone cares but we tend to track these things to keep the scales balanced. One friend drives two hours to visit all the time, while the other friend does not. One friend brings food when visiting; the other does not. One friend initiates the calls; the other friend does not.

To an extent, it makes logical sense why we want to track these tit-for-tat actions; if the scales aren't balanced, it could mean we're getting taken advantage of. The problem is when we let these tit-for-tat actions determine our choices. Again, it is based on arbitrary or misguided assessments that only hold our own limited perspective. A better solution is to simply have boundaries as to what we will and won't do or give and stop worrying about the scores.

Assume that we had a crystal ball and could see that the friend who never initiates calls or contact loves us dearly. Would we still feel upset about being the one to reach out first? We have to know that these tit-for-tat situations cannot be used to judge one's level of affection. They can however help us understand their tendencies and if we don't like those tendencies, then we will grow apart.

Bad Friendships and Growing Apart

If we shouldn't use our friendship meter to determine how much affection and giving our friend has shown us, what can we do to determine if it's a good or bad friendship? And what if our friend really cares for us but is debilitating for us, like an alcohol or drug addiction, for example. This type of negative dynamic is exactly what a bad friendship is: a mutually caring friendship that has bad effects or bad influences.

It doesn't matter how much we care, and it doesn't matter how much they care. If there are bad effects, there are bad effects that need to be rectified. The amount we care provides only an indicator of what we're willing to do about the bad effects and how we address our friend.

For example, if we have a really strong friendship but our friend is doing something that we no longer approve of, we have to let them know and establish boundaries about what we're willing to do around them. It doesn't mean we have to grow apart; we just draw a line in the sand as to what we won't stand for or let affect us negatively.

Aside from bad friendships, maybe we simply don't want to be that close anymore. Maybe we're not meshing with our friend well anymore. Instead of going out to party every day like we used to, we'd rather stay home and our friend hates that. Or maybe our friend has constant drama that we're tired of being a listening ear or helping hand for. Maybe we just can't get over some of their tendencies, like the fact that they don't reach out to us enough.

In all cases, growing apart is our choice and it should be a deliberate one. Setting boundaries is something we must actively choose to do. This, again, doesn't mean we don't care; it just means we are changing. We should embrace our own feelings, set boundaries and be unapologetic about it.

Time Lapse

It seems, however, that despite the fact we think we can care for someone deeply and not talk to or hang out with them much, there is an instinctive need for continuous connection to those we care about. If we truly care about someone, it's hard to accept that our feelings would eventually change due to time alone.

In a depressing example, what if our close friend passed away? Would our feelings for them slowly change? Our instinctive answer is "no way," but the intense anger and sadness of losing a loved one needs to subside over time or we wouldn't be able to continue with our own lives. We may love them the same but the impact of emotional situations, people and events will morph as time goes by.

Imagine falling in love, truly believing this person is forever, only to break up and find another true love later on. There is something in our makeup that helps us to move on, to continue to change and grow. It is likely no different with regard to friendships. If a friend isn't around at all, even if we cared dearly for them, after a while, the strength of those memories and associated feelings will likely subside unless we are actively working to keep them.

Communicate and Create

Assuming that we've determined we want to keep a strong friendship and we don't want to grow apart, there are two things we simply have to do: communicate and create new memories. We have to communicate because we may not know what our friend wants or needs. They may need affection in a way that we aren't showing. This is how we replace our broken friendship meter. We talk to them and get an idea as to what they'd appreciate.

We create new memories by interacting, of course. We determine what things they like or what issues we may have collectively and give in relation to our own feelings of affection. When we do things for them based on our own level of affection, while taking into consideration their needs, we create a natural balance that isn't dependent on guesswork. It's what we discuss together or what we want for ourselves. For most close friendships, this type of dynamic happens automatically. But sometimes life gets in the way and we need to be more assertive about it.

Shared Goals and Life

Friendships are not meant to be difficult, but it is no surprise that life just happens. Life seems to be the indirect cause of a lot of inactive friendships. In these cases, we have to make it a point to reach out and hang out or do something with them. Many of us seem to be less than good at this, letting life's priorities take control, while some of our best friends and times get put on the back burner. It may ultimately take a concerted effort by both parties but only one person is needed to initiate that effort.

One thing that can help incorporate life into a friendship is to find common collaborative goals or passions. Chances are that there was originally something in our lives that acted as this shared goal: school, work, a sport, a particular event or venue. Having a new shared goal can be a great way to keep the friendship strong and can last through life's obstacles.

Life happens but one thing that we have heard, time and again, from those on their deathbeds is that friends and family are usually top of the list. This, however, is NOT a reason to keep friends that we no longer feel a connection to or that infringe on our boundaries. But for those who make the cut, let's be better at involving them in our lives where possible, to find shared goals and keep our friendships strong if not for them, for ourselves.

Boundaries and the Average of Five People

In relationships, we are often subtly (or overtly) changing with the person or people we are surrounded by. Why is this? The misguided cliché, you are the average of the five people you spend the most time around seems to come from this general dynamic. The reality is that we are constantly adjusting to improve our interactions or to get what we want out of the interaction. It's like being on a sports team; we have to adjust to our teammates. Yet is Michael Jordan the average of five people? Bill Gates? Jeff Bezos? Let's address this rule and talk about why establishing boundaries can help us.

Cum Hoc Ergo Propter Hoc

First off, there will always be many correlations that are true about the people we spend the most time around. We choose to spend time around people for various reasons. If we happen to smoke, then likely there's going to be a smoker in our group. If we love talking about sports, there's likely someone who loves talking about sports in the group. If we're a billionaire, chances are there would be more rich people in the group.

Taking that concept to the extreme is what we get when we talk about the average of five people. People are cutting off friends and family, searching for mentors, positive and rich people to hang around to network and increase their average. This may work for some but aside from being disingenuous, it also isn't the most reasonable thing to do.

What we have to remember is "cum hoc ergo propter hoc," or for those not aspiring to learn Latin or be like Nietzsche, *correlation does not imply causation.* Being around these people isn't typically the reason we are successful, or positive, or smokers, or into sports. Unfortunately, this logical fallacy is often overlooked. It is very difficult in many cases to prove causation in certain types of statistics and we need to be wary of this as it could have us focusing on the wrong thing.

We're Average, on Average

Imagine that we are in high school or college and we really want to be a good basketball player. So, we decide to hang around good basketball players in hopes that their success and skills would somehow rub off on us. We want to be the average of them. If anyone said that, we'd laugh them out of the room. Clearly, we'd need to put in the work; we'd have to actually work at being a better basketball player. There would be a good chance if we did get better that we would end up friends with some of them, making the average rule true.

Not only that but on average, when we finally do make the team, we'd likely be the average of the players we play with. It is no different in terms of any other life concept or situation; whatever we do, whether it is good, bad or indifferent, puts us in some average category, on average. The average of five people rule is no different; it is a somewhat meaningless statistic that says we're average, on average.

Bad Influences and Bad Hands

But what about bad influences? Imagine for a second that we are teenagers. We're growing up with friends that are constantly in trouble with the law, stealing, doing extreme drugs and causing general mischief but we get along great with them. Or what if we are growing up with a family that is negative and hateful?

These influences definitely could have a negative impact on our lives and this is also the contrary reason the average of five is often cited, so we can purge the negative out of our lives. Let's quickly unpack why these situations could have a negative impact on our lives.

If we are hanging around friends that have or did something illegal, we could get arrested right along with them, even if we didn't do anything. We could get roped into trying extreme drugs through peer pressure. Maybe we start to see drugs and illegal activities as a norm, which makes us more likely to do them in the future.

What about if we grew up in a negative, hateful family? What is the influence of consistently hearing negative, hateful things? The fear is that we start to take on those same traits, that we start to become what we observe consistently. Like an echo chamber, we are only hearing and seeing things that support the negative, hateful things.

Adjusting to the Team

In some ways, with respect to all of our interactions, we are always naturally adjusting to reduce and eliminate conflict, to make our interactions easier and more fruitful, or to achieve certain goals. Our team is the five people or our friends and families. Since we are around them the most, it makes sense that we are going to adjust to their actions, their styles of communication and their beliefs.

Even if we have strong beliefs, our thoughts are often slowly molded by the things in our immediate environment. It is clear, however, that doesn't have to be the case; we just have to be very deliberate. Can we have close friends or family that don't share our political beliefs? That don't share our religious beliefs? That don't share our goals? That don't make the same money?

Of course, we'd say yes to all of the above; we can have close friends and family that don't believe or do the same things we do. We have to make sure we draw a line in the sand and firmly establish what we want and believe and more importantly, protect it accordingly.

Boundaries

That line in the sand is our boundaries. It's protecting what we are or are not willing to do and believe. Boundaries protect our goals, ensuring that we take actions in accordance with our own goals and beliefs instead of others. When we are dealing with others, having strong boundaries allows us to navigate without being negatively influenced.

If, for example, we were against our friends doing extreme drugs or stealing and causing mischief, then we should have a boundary that doesn't let us or them cross it. If we are friends and don't approve, are we telling them how stupid it is? Are we making sure they don't do anything like that while we're around? Are we making sure they have nothing illegal on them when we hang out? Of course, if we started doing that, there's a good chance at least a few of the friends would stop coming around because of our nagging rules.

In the case of our hateful family, we'd establish a boundary about not hating or being negative the way they do. We'd learn to put ourselves in a physical or mental space to ensure we understand deeply how to never get to that level of hate and negativity.

Wanting It Bad Enough

Boundaries are not only important for extreme situations but for everyday relationships and ourselves. If we have important beliefs or things we want to do, we have to establish a boundary around them. Without boundaries, those in our lives, those we work with and even ourselves have no idea what is or isn't a priority.

Take a simple example of working out. If working out is very important to us, then we'd need to establish a boundary relating to working out. It means that nothing is going to keep us from doing that to a reasonable extent. If it's our time to work out and a friend wants to hang out, with boundaries protecting our workout goals, we'd tell them we can go afterward or another day.

If we don't protect our goals, we'll find achieving them to be difficult. This is often a silent killer making us or others think we don't want it bad enough, yet, in reality, we just need to be smarter about establishing these boundaries.

Bad Boundaries

Not all boundaries are good, however. They can cause a lot of arguments and issues as well. If it's a simple case of a missed happy hour, maybe that's ok; but what if we miss our anniversary because of our boundary of nothing impacting our workout schedule? What if we miss out on our child growing up because of some other boundary around our obsession?

The obsessed entrepreneur, the closed-off partner, the hard-headed child — in some ways, these individuals are all simply establishing boundaries to protect things that they find important. Maybe they were forced to assert themselves because of a bad environment they grew up in, or maybe they have lofty goals.

When establishing boundaries, maybe they are too extreme or too subtle; we should be constantly reassessing and updating them as we interact. Every social interaction includes navigating boundaries and as such, when we encounter conflicts, we should take that as a time to re-assess and ensure our boundaries are appropriate.

Conflict and Assessing Boundaries

One of the easiest ways to assess our boundaries is when we argue or have conflict in a social interaction. Imagine that we are *fighting over the little things* and we find that we are starting to get emotional. We want to avoid an uncontrollable argument, so we decide to stop and walk away. Yet the person we are walking away from is also starting to get upset because we are walking away. In that instance, we should ask ourselves a few questions:

1. Whose boundary is it? If we walk away when an argument starts to get heated, clearly, it's our boundary, right? They are encroaching on "our" space. Well, not necessarily. All interactions involve everyone's boundaries, which means that even though we are walking away, the person we are walking away from has their own boundaries that could be telling them they shouldn't be letting this go. Understanding both boundaries to an extent will help us to learn:

2. What is the boundary protecting? In the argument scenario, we are walking away to protect ourselves from getting overemotional and starting an uncontrollable argument. Yet we have to also try to understand the boundary of the person we are interacting with. What is it they are trying to protect by not letting go? We won't know the answer for sure but we can at least acknowledge that it is important to them. Ideally, we find out by asking them why or what their issue is. That then can lead us to our final question:

3. Is there a better way? Once we have an idea of whose boundary is protecting what, we can start to understand if we can or should change our own boundary to accommodate. For instance, if our rule is to just walk away and we find out our significant other needs to know we care about the issue, we can change our rule to always tell them before we walk away. We could ensure that we tell them we care and we'd be open to discussing it at a particular date and time after we calm down.

Acknowledge the Consequences

Sometimes, after assessing our boundaries, we decide we don't want to change anything and that is perfectly fine; we just have to acknowledge the consequences. If we never go out with our friend because of our crazy workout schedule, we may lose a friend if they don't adapt. If we don't want to adapt to certain boundaries for people in our lives, we may lose them in some way.

Losing favor with others is often the result of boundaries, which is why it is important to use them wisely and constantly reassess. We may end up surrounded by similar people. We may end up the average of the five people we spend the most time with, but it's not the reason we are where we are; it's only a correlation and a pretty meaningless one at that. The reason we are where we are is the result of our established boundaries and the work we've put in.

P.S.

The dynamic of losing friends and family members is difficult to accept and acknowledge and can cause us to become afraid to establish boundaries at all. But we should never be afraid to establish boundaries to protect what is important to us. If we don't, we will lose much more than the favor of our friends and our family; we will lose ourselves.

DAY TO DAY

"The important thing is not to stop questioning.
Curiosity has its own reason for existing."
-Albert Einstein

Trolling for Insecurities, Flaws and Weaknesses

Who are the trolls? Who are the people who supposedly seem to love bringing others down, trash-talking, laughing "at" someone versus "with" someone? Come to think about it, who are the hecklers in a crowd at sporting events, political events, or comedy shows, trying to get into someone else's head, piss them off, or elicit some response? Oh wait, lots of us trash-talk when we play sports. And many of us have said something hurtful to our own loved ones when we argue. Are trolls and hecklers really that far from the norm? And what if all they are doing is underscoring our own insecurities and weaknesses?

Trash-Talking

We all know the person who loves to trash-talk (or maybe we're that person). Some of the best athletes are also the biggest trash-talkers. For anyone who plays sports, we all seem to do it for slightly different reasons but arguably, the main two are either: 1) Get into someone else's head (for various reasons) or 2) Boost ourselves up.

If we're battling someone, whether it's a sport or any other type of competition, we're giving it our all. We're analyzing their every move, their flaws, their strengths and when we find something, we aim to capitalize on it. Let's say we're playing a basketball player who is extremely good at shooting three-point shots, so we tell them, "You couldn't dribble past my grandmother." We constantly goad them to take the ball in, which is exactly what we want.

This trash-talk expands into the stands where fans are goading each other the same way. Generally, in sports, it's all in good fun. However, some people seem to take it too far and that's when fights occur. The problem is "too far" is different for every single person.

Going Too Far

It's tough when we hear about negative things happening due to bullying or some form of trolling. It's completely unacceptable, yet there's a problem with our traditional method of addressing the problem. We often look to make our words politically correct. We attempt to please everyone by always walking the line, not saying anything that could possibly hurt someone else's feelings.

The problem is that when we operate this way for too long, we go too far in the other direction. On one hand, we've solved trash-talking, bullying and trolling but then, on the other, we create a society that can only speak their minds in secret, likely harboring a lot more problems in the long run.

One person might be triggered by a racial slur even if there was no malice behind the term. Another person may be triggered by curse words. Another person may be triggered by a prayer. The point is, there is no easy line to tell us when things are too far and as such, the concept of freedom of speech regardless of what that speech is must remain.

While we can typically agree that anyone spouting false statements knowingly is pretty low, how often are they really just someone's opinion? Is there anything we can do to stop it? Should we? And if not, what are our options?

Social Conflict

Social interactions all have a purpose or meaning that is derived, requiring that we take action (to include inaction). As long as we're ok with the interaction and we don't feel the need to beat the other person in some way and don't need to boost ourselves up for some reason, there is a pretty low chance we'll feel any desire to trash-talk anyone.

Yet, the moment that changes, the moment we get into a conflict, it becomes something that we need to win. Once that happens, things quickly escalate and attempts to manipulate start to come out. It doesn't matter if it's a friend, a family member, or a stranger; if our need to win is larger than our desire to keep the peace, there's a good chance we're going to target someone's insecurities and weaknesses.

When we're arguing with someone and target their insecurities, it could come out very naturally, as if we've been analyzing social interactions our entire lives (go figure). With arguments and social conflict, if we aren't careful and learn to manage our emotions, very instinctual patterns arise. In many cases, we aren't even intentionally picking on someone else.

Bullies

Cyberbullying and "IRL" bullying are the same concept. It seems pretty closely related to trolling, yet generally, it's when things are escalated, persistent, or cause physical harm. But when a bully beats another person up, what are they gaining from it? Did they just want to emphasize that the other person was stupid or lame? To who? What's the point? It's no different than our other conflicts — get into someone's head (for various reasons) or boost themselves up.

What we want to underscore here is that, regardless of the bully's reasoning, it's very obvious they seem to have a knack for identifying weaknesses, flaws and insecurities.

Not only are they pros at identifying weaknesses but they are also deliberately choosing their victims based on those weaknesses, whereas an athlete is doing it in sport and the rest of us are doing it in conjunction with general social interactions that occur (or groupthink ... which we won't address today...).

Intent to Troll

We're going to classify a troll as anyone who is intentionally targeting another person's weaknesses, flaws, or insecurities, regardless of the purpose or result. That means that whether the trolling is good or bad is subjective. It completely depends on the person or group being trolled. For example, someone who trolls a spam caller would probably be considered a good troll, but what about someone who trolls for a political purpose?

What about trolls that are doing it for humor or satire? Are they good or bad? What about a troll who says false things versus a troll that says true things? The bottom line is we know that trolling is nothing new — defamation and hecklers have been around since the dawn of man. The likelihood of us being able to fix it and make them go away is zero. So why not find something we can use to our advantage if it's going to be here?

The Troll Advantage

Trolling is here to stay; there may be some who have no ill intent, whereas others have nothing but ill intent. Yet, in all cases, we know at least that the bottom line is that they target our weaknesses, flaws and insecurities. That means that we can use trolls to our advantage.

If there's something that a troll says that completely enrages us or hits that nerve just right, know they are on to us. They've seen through something and pinpointed a weakness or an insecurity. Even if whatever they are saying isn't true, if it strikes a chord, there's something about it that worries us, something that needs to be hardened or worked on.

So next time we encounter a troll that strikes that chord just right, please don't "feel sorry" for them like so many people like to say. We have no idea what the troll's intent was. Instead, take it in, learn, improve and harden ourselves until we can ignore, laugh, or heck, troll them back.

Experience Versus Book Smarts

Mike Tyson was the youngest person to ever win the heavyweight championship at 20 years old. Mark Zuckerberg launched Facebook at 19. Kailash Satyarthi survived an assassination attempt at 15 and won the Nobel Peace Prize by 20. There are lots of examples of "inexperienced" people doing extremely amazing things. They must have worked hard; they probably tried things and failed a lot behind closed doors. No one would call Tyson a book-smart person but he certainly understood the book of boxing.

Experience Over Books

Experience always wins over book smarts; we all generally agree with this. If we want to learn how to do a backflip, chances are book knowledge won't help us much. We can read about techniques, about where to move, how to position ourselves, we can even watch others do it. Yet, for some reason, until we actually do it, there are often things we just don't understand or anticipate without experiencing.

Many subject areas seem to rely heavily on experience. For example, try to explain what getting into a fight is like to someone who hasn't fought before. Any explanation would not likely do it justice. Yet, there is the opposite as well; think math or really anything that relies primarily on some form of cognition and imagination. Any constructs that are heavily involved with cognition and less involved with the physical senses sounds a lot more book-like, doesn't it? Or does it?

What Is a Book?

A book is a bunch of words on pieces of paper. With Audible, a book is someone talking to us. With YouTube, a book is someone showing us. The point is that these are just different mediums through which we take in someone's thoughts, experiences or expression. When someone is book smart, that means they are reflecting or taking in experiences through a different medium.

Yet, it's not only passive intake. We have to think about the information critically and we have to apply it for it to be truly learned. This is why anyone can easily read a difficult book or watch a complex video but have a very hard time understanding it. Reading a book without any thought is like watching an MMA match and thinking we can fight.

For some topics, we don't need (or want) the experience — for example, a bad encounter from a bad breakup, to accidents, injuries, disabilities, starvation and death. In these scenarios, we don't need the experience to know it sucks. We can read, watch, listen and empathize and strategically come up with actions based on those thoughts.

Compressed Experiences

The idea of empathy plus strategy, the ability to look at any situation, the ability to read any book and come up with scenarios as to why certain actions would or wouldn't be advantageous is really what we are referring to with book smarts.

Imagine this. A baseball is heading toward our chest. It's not going fast but it won't feel good to get hit in the chest. We decide to move out of the way and catch the ball instead of letting it hit us. The act of moving and catching is all an estimation. Before it happens, it's all made up in our minds before we act. If we have experience catching a baseball or with sports at all, it probably will come naturally. If not, we may not even attempt to catch the ball and let it fly instead.

Everything we do is a matter of using the information in our minds to predict future actions and reactions; it's all in our heads. Being book smart is when we have no direct experiences but can think about it, imagine it and come up with strategies based on our imagination and thoughts. The main reason books don't compare to experiences is because we can't paint a picture with the same level of fidelity as the real thing. It's like a compressed version of experience. If we had read about this baseball scenario just before the actual event occurred, what's the likelihood we would've been slightly more prepared? We can't operate optimally without both.

Arguing with Experience

It's said that Mike Tyson religiously watched boxing film when he was training as a kid. He was reading the book of boxing, all while training extensively. If Tyson didn't study tapes extensively, how successful would he have been?

If someone had more experience fighting than him and wanted to teach him something, how would they do it? When he's already a 20-year-old champion, why should he even listen to someone else's experiences? Assuming just showing or telling him didn't work, the key is they'd have to find a common link or figure out what he has and hasn't experienced directly and what he knows through other book-smart mediums.

Arguing that they have experience would mean nothing to Tyson. They'd have to provide experiences he can relate to and weave them into their reasoning. This is no different whether talking to an open-minded thinker, a teenager going through puberty or an annoying, know-it-all boss. And if we happen to run into a brick wall, well, we've already talked about how to deal with that...

Street-Smart Caveat

As we've alluded to, book smarts are anything in our thoughts outside of actual experience. Some like Gary Vaynerchuk aren't readers but are still massively successful and likely strong critical thinkers when it comes to assessing their problems. They likely have a strong ability to correlate their experiences and make predictions and conclusions from their experiences alone.

This idea of street smarts is experience plus our own smarts. Normally book smarts are based on someone else's thoughts and experiences. Why can't it be our own? We can read our own book and analyze it over and over. So, I shamelessly include this type of thinking process or introspection as book smart but that isn't totally fair. We have to underscore that experience is the equivalent of doing. Until we do something, until we try something, we get nowhere.

Vastness of the World

There are thousands of different careers, thousands of different sports, billions of people and thousands of religions. We simply can't experience it all. The idea that book smarts can't cut it runs contrary to this vastness as well. If experience didn't go hand in hand with book smarts, we'd be extinct by now.

If we think about most subjects despite the vastness, they all bleed into other subjects. That means when we have experience in one area, we automatically gain some level of experience in many other areas. If, for example, we have experience working as an IT support technician, there are likely a high number of jobs or careers that we can relate to. Having that small link allows us to use book smarts to then move into other areas or understand other concepts.

Books Are Cheat Codes

Einstein is estimated to have taken almost 10 years to come up with the theory of relativity. Now, we can see not only the fruits of his labor but it can be taught in a single class and summarized in a single YouTube video. We can learn in hours what it took someone else years to learn. This effect is seen time and time again over the years of human existence.

This may have something to do with why some of the most successful people in the world advocate reading a LOT— Oprah Winfrey, Bill Gates, Warren Buffett, Elon Musk, etc.

So, next time you think of a book-smart nerd, don't forget to include Mike Tyson and many of the other inexperienced but successful people.

Work, "Working" or *Working*

When was the last time you went to work but didn't do much "working"? Have you or your co-worker slept on the job? Have you or your co-worker been on social media for the better part of the day? Have you or your co-worker watched YouTube for more than just a few minutes while you were on the clock? You aren't alone...

The Enabling Job

This phenomenon isn't anything new; it's just more in our face. We have more options. Instead of socializing with whoever is around us, who may be actually *working*, we can socialize on our phones. In an enabling job, there is no immediate feedback on work tasks and if there is, it is not significant enough to push someone to take action.

An enabling job could look like this: Get to work anywhere between 7 and 9 a.m. and socialize with co-workers sitting around you. Prepare for a status meeting from 10–11 a.m. Talk about the status of your work and how long it will take to finish, then listen to 10 other people give their status. Leave the meeting a little late, socialize with your co-workers that were in the meeting, then go to lunch. Get back around 1 p.m.

and catch up on social media, prepare for another meeting from 2–3 p.m. Afterwards, possibly do an hour of work, then go home.

Of course, there are plenty of jobs that don't allow that much spare time. In a busy restaurant, most employees don't have much time to do anything but serve customers. In most busy jobs, there isn't much ability to slack without looking like a complete jerk. In these busy jobs, there is a constant stream of tasks that typically provide immediate (and significant) feedback.

There's not much chance to do anything if there's always another customer requiring assistance. Imagine a call center that has a caller every minute — there just wouldn't ever be enough time in the day to do anything. Yet, even in some of these environments, plenty of workers are going slow, ignoring customers to check their phone or socialize with others. In these jobs, the feedback may be immediate but it's not significant enough to matter. Yet if the job does provide immediate and significant feedback all the time, how would they know the workers aren't overworked? How would they know the workers aren't milking the system?

Why Does it Matter?

Plenty of companies squeeze every ounce of work out of their workers and it's simply too much (cough...Amazon). Yet in some areas, the opposite tends to be happening, yielding lazy workers (cough...the government). Aside from those extremes and maybe a few customers or managers being annoyed, it doesn't really matter. In fact, if we reduce stress and get enjoyment out of life by relaxing at work a bit, then so be it. It's somewhat the equivalent of some societies closing shop a few hours in the middle of the day to relax/sleep/socialize. No one wants to be stressed all the time and who are we to determine what the optimal amount of work is?

The human mind is very adaptable and seems to have some sort of lazy gene (or efficiency gene). There's always an inclination to do the least amount of work to get whatever it wants. So, the average worker will do the tasks needed to get paid, do those tasks right such that they can keep getting paid without threat of anything happening to their job. Once they get the minimum done, they are free to do whatever they want, all while still getting paid. It only makes sense to do this.

Yet, being lazy can also lead to the best workers. For example, the best workers often end up doing more than the average worker by being as efficient as possible. In doing so, they get more work done in less time and look better than the rest, making them more likely to get a promotion or be highly regarded. Why don't we all do this then? What's the right way?

Priorities

The thing is, it all boils down to our own priorities. These priorities may be conscious (e.g., gimme a raise) or unconscious (e.g., gimme the dopamine). There is an infinite number of possible priorities for each of us and the priorities guide us to our most likely course of action at work. If our desire for a raise is strong, that will at least make us aware of what we *think* it takes to get that raise. (Whether we are thinking the right things or not is another story.)

If we have no real conscious priority with regard to our job aside from "get paid and go home," there's a really good chance we will do the minimum and not much more. If our priority is to become the manager, then there's a really good chance we are going to try to do more than someone who doesn't have that priority.

Again, there's nothing wrong with having the priority of getting paid and going home. In fact, many of today's work environments are built to reinforce this bare minimum mentality.

Hourly (and Salary) Implosion

Good employers have a tough role to balance; they are trying to get the most amount of work out of their employees, while simultaneously providing the best employment situation (pay, benefits, leave, demands, etc.). Of course, this all depends on the business's revenue; if the business doesn't make much, it can't give much back to the employees. To make more revenue, the employees have to do more and more work; this dynamic always results in opposing forces.

The thing is, hourly and salary wages in many environments can cause some strange effects. If, for example, we pay a worker $10 an hour to be a cashier but there are zero customers, the business goes down. So, we have to bring in enough customers to cover that cost. Because the market rate for the worker (or possibly minimum wage) is $10/hour, then we have a set minimum we need to operate the business. In doing so, in some cases, we impact the ability of a business to get started, as well as the ability for a business to stay in business.

Then, to add to the mix, if we have a typical hourly or salaried worker, there is no simple incentive structure that exists. The best workers get paid the same as the worst workers, constantly creating a dynamic of infighting and high school drama because "Suzie comes in late every day," "Joe barely does anything," and "Lance gets paid more than everyone."

The concept of hourly or salary in a lot of jobs seems to be perpetuating the problem, unintentionally "incentivizing" bare minimum and lowering standards, all the while being unhinged from the actual customer and revenue.

Do Work, Get Paid, Relax

While there isn't anything wrong with relaxing on the job, we should get paid based on what we contribute to the greatest extent possible. In sales, for example, if we sell, we get a commission; if we don't sell, we don't get anything. It's as simple as that. General day-to-day work should be carved up in a similar fashion, such that not doing work equates to not getting paid. This may sound extreme, but the idea is similar to farming, hunting and many of the timeless jobs of the past.

Of course, before too many hands go up, this is definitely waaaaay easier said than done. Firstly, we can't track tasks and output easily. It often isn't like sales where one sale equates to one dollar. Not to mention, there's an extremely large number of things that could go wrong with the structure if not done well. From extreme work conditions to workers gaming the system, to unfair pay structures and plenty more, the problems are endless. The typical do work, get paid sounds like a dictator that wants to squeeze out every ounce of work, which is definitely NOT the answer or the point.

Regardless of both the positives or negatives, changes are coming whether we like it or not. We may, one day, start seeing streaming pay, where every second we work, our account increases. With AI and more tracking methods on the horizon, the hourly and salary wages as we know them could slowly disappear, for better or worse.

Let's keep thinking about wages and revolutionizing the ideas now so we don't end up repeating some of the historical labor tragedies of years past.

Everyone Must Have
a Business

Imagine you love video games. You work to survive, of course, but ultimately to buy and play video games. It's not like you have any business aspirations involving gaming. You just love the experience of playing video games and chatting and interacting with others who do the same. What if we told you that doesn't matter and that you need to have a business? The funny thing is, we all have businesses; we just don't register as one. Put on your non-biased thinking cap and let's chat.

Death and Taxes

First things first, this is for capitalistic societies where tax laws are built around capitalistic tendencies. In these areas, it is to our disadvantage to not run a business. For those who hate taxes and are always using the death and taxes quote, we have to realize that, at least in the U.S., the original point was to push us all to somehow add to the economic ecosystem by performing income-producing activities. If we perform these income-producing activities, we are helping the economy and also deducting from whatever income we would normally be making, hence reducing the amount of taxes we end up paying.

In a business, for example, hypothetically, all of its income could go right back into expenses to continue to produce or attempt to produce income and as such, have nothing left for income taxes. How the government would still make its money, of course, is through what we all know and love well: sales and property taxes, which are forms of consumption taxes.

But, if we look at general income tax brackets, we'll see anything from 10% up to almost 40%. Imagine making one million dollars and having $400,000 shaved off the top for the taxman. Well, if we aren't producing anything with all that money, the system is kind of saying, "If you don't use it, we will." Even as a gamer working at GameStop, bringing in $10,000 a year could benefit from not giving away 10% of the income earned. Who wouldn't want to save $1,000?

Video Gamer = No Business?

Great, so, we all can agree that having a business could save us up to 10% on our income taxes. But, how can a video gamer be a business? Well, first off, the easy analogy is Fortnite gamer, Ninja.

For those who don't know Fortnite or haven't heard of the gamer, Ninja, at one time, he made $500,000 a month in just Twitch donations. This was verifiable by just watching his streams where the donations could be seen rolling in.

Of course, we aren't Ninja and the chances of going that viral isn't high at all. However, that doesn't mean we can't set everything up as a business anyway. If we live-stream on Twitch, it should be set up to accept gifts. Those gifts should be sent to the business. If we want to have sponsors, we should have sponsors pay the business. Whenever we purchase gaming-related items as a verifiable part of the business, it should also be purchased by the business.

Personal Brand + Consumer

Another term that may or may not induce vomiting at this point is "personal brand." Love or hate the idea, we have to admit that Gary Vaynerchuk and many others are right: marketing has become available to everyone to an extreme extent because of our mobile devices and social media to the extent that now everyone *is* their own personal brand, whether we decide to do anything with it or not.

Everyone has a personal brand and as such, they have attention from others that can sell or be sold. That means we are all essentially tiny marketing businesses to large companies. We are no longer only consumers; we are both brands/marketing and consumers.

For those skeptics out there, if it feels like a stretch, that may have been the case 10 years ago but not anymore. Let's take a small group of 100 followers. If our video game Twitch stream has 100 somewhat-engaged followers, how easy is it for them to be influenced by the next game we play? What about the gear we decide to purchase and use? What about the related topics we consistently discuss? Over a year of following, does that sound like it could result in $50-100 of purchases per follower? That means we could influence up to 100 people to make up to $10,000 in purchases in a year. Whether we decide to take a percentage of that or not (profit versus non-profit), we are still doing business, just not as explicitly as we are used to.

The big companies know this. That's why they sell to the influencers who then speak to the followers more directly. To reach a million people, these big companies now only have to reach 10,000 influencers with 100 people. That's usually waaaay cheaper than trying to do that in their own direct campaign and can reduce costs by over a factor of 10 times, all from a bunch of random gamers with 100 people following them.

Morals Shmorals

Ok, we have to admit, in some ways, it seems kind of messed up. Our friends and followers are constantly being influenced and sold things. In sales, they always teach to sell to our friends and families first and if we believe in the product, then we're doing them a favor. But no matter how much we may believe that, putting business pressure on friends and families feels wrong if it's not done just right. If we blatantly ask everyone to purchase cell phones through our company, unless we can give them a verifiable deal over any other company, it wouldn't seem genuine. Also, if we ask them to purchase when they don't need a new cell phone, it also can feel disingenuous or like undue pressure.

How many of us have bought something from a friend or family member, not because we needed or wanted it but because they were our friend?

Enter personal brand. The thing about a personal brand is it's always on, meaning if we sell things via our personal brand, we are selling to those who are our friends and family, giving it the same feel as those typical sales courses. Who wants to see constant sales on our Instagram feed every day? "There goes Joe again trying to sell his workout supplements…"

Content Over Sales

Ideally, things should be so well integrated that it is all about the content and interacting with our followers. We should make content for ourselves and for our followers, not for the purpose of selling. Content should be for the purpose of adding value. Then, if by nature of enjoying the content, our followers want to purchase whatever we have available, then so be it.

That's a fine line that often doesn't feel like it yields business success. On Instagram, Joe can currently sell more supplements if it's an obvious, straightforward sell than if he only talked about his workout regime and its benefits with links in his description.

Yet, are Joe's followers more or less engaged than someone who focuses on content first? Gary Vaynerchuk is one of those who push content over sales and to provide as much value as possible, garnering as much attention as possible before even thinking about sales, playing a patience game.

Is that the right answer for small businesses? Is there still a problem with everything still ultimately leading to sales? Maybe, maybe not but one thing is for sure: it definitely feels better to focus on passion and content than it does to focus on sales.

Back to Business

We all need to have a business for two main reasons: 1) to save at least 10% on our taxes and 2) to be prepared for the possibility that our personal brand and our existing passions have the potential to give something of value to others.

If we feel bad and don't like making money off of our friends and family, why do we purchase anything at all? Would we truly rather purchase from strangers than people we know?

The tribal Internet landscape is coming; our local market is going to be the realm of our social media tribes. There may be a point where we can easily purchase our supplements from Joe, our skincare products from Mary and our clothes from Susan. Amazon may still exist as a major broker just as Facebook but the exchange of goods and services could be the brands we follow and participate with regularly, not the typical large conglomerates that we have no real ties to.

For those who aren't into business, focus on just creating something of value for others by doing what we love. The interesting thing is that for anyone looking for purpose or meaning in life, that's one very easy and real way to do it. If we provide some small bit of value to others, it makes us a part of something larger than ourselves.

We all have our own business; we just don't always make it official. Let's make it official and register our businesses. The business will be a reminder to live life by always trying to give value to others, even if we just play video games to do it.

Taking on a Lead Role

Imagine you are newly promoted to lead a small team responsible for getting an important task done. If this task doesn't get done right, people could get hurt. Being in the lead position means you bear the responsibility of making sure the task is accomplished most efficiently while minimizing the risk of anyone getting hurt. You hear from your predecessor that one of the team members is never there, always has excuses and seems to do their own thing. They tell you that they should be talked to as soon as possible before they end up causing a real problem. How do you handle this?

Set Rules up Front?

Some may try to establish some rules up front; there are many recommendations out there that emphasize that. In new management positions or leadership roles, we are supposed to set clear expectations and lay down the law before anyone gets comfortable with us. Want a team to take us seriously? Emphasizing the areas we are serious about in the beginning is the general rule.

Let's even go out on a limb and assume that our predecessor was someone we knew and trusted well. We understand their general way of thinking and leading. We agree with their principles and believe that if we had to make a bet, everything they are saying about the situation would be the same as we would assess ourselves. Emphasizing their suggestions up front, before anything else, would make even more sense.

However, there is a catch. We need to recognize that even if the recommendations of our predecessor are spot on, even if certain things should be established as soon as possible, there's something else we should do first.

Team Connection

Even if our predecessor told us everything we need to know, the team doesn't know us. They haven't connected with us at all. We could make the perfect calls every day but if we didn't work to establish a connection, there would likely be something missing when tough situations occur.

We aren't advocating for getting into the weeds of someone's personal life, who they are dating, or what president they voted for. Instead, we want to find out what makes the team member excel and what their goals are in relation to the team. Are there things in their personal life that affect these goals? Do they have other personal goals that conflict with the team's goals? Is their team role effective? How do they interact with other team members?

Talking to the team to understand these areas firsthand *before* establishing rules and expectations is a great way to start earning respect. If we set rules and expectations before we've even spoken to them on an individual level, we are ignoring their thoughts and feelings. Doing so can be a very negative precedent to establish (unless we want robots).

Respect Bank

If we ignore our team's thoughts and feelings, we are taking for granted that little thing called respect. Many leads and managers demand respect without even knowing it. Whenever we establish rules before a team gets to know us, we are asking them for respect but on loan, like credit. We are saying, "You don't know me and I don't know you but follow me anyway and do x, y and z." Asking anyone to follow us without providing anything in return is a good way to start off on the wrong foot.

What leadership should do instead is give respect to others by making sure everyone has a voice. Ask everyone for input and see how they operate firsthand. Ask questions on a very basic level and get to know everyone. Establish that changes may come but only after we've done our homework and worked with everyone to understand individual needs. At no point should someone's first day look like a list of demands, rules, or expectations unless they've already worked with everyone in some form.

For large teams where it is unreasonable to expect the leader to know everyone's individual strengths and weaknesses, that means that the team needs more leaders and more groups. A lead with 100 team members needs to separate things into groups such that the primary touchpoints are a manageable number, 10 groups of 10, for example. Smartly dividing things is a key way to connect efficiently with the team.

Establish Responsibilities

Every team member should have a role, an area that they focus on and are responsible for. The best teams will have roles and responsibilities seamlessly interconnected. On a baseball field, for example, each player on the field is keeping track of their area of responsibility. If they don't, players could literally step on each other, trying to catch a ball. It is no different on teams. If those areas aren't well defined, team members will be stepping over each other, or they won't be well utilized.

In some situations, general responsibilities are already defined but sometimes redundant due to the size of tasks that need to be handled. In these cases, we need to then go to a more granular level of detail. There shouldn't be any team member who doesn't have something they are fully responsible for (this includes juniors and apprentices).

These responsibilities also should take into consideration individual strengths and weaknesses. The lead needs to account for all of these factors and always help everyone understand the why behind what is being done.

Direction Without Directing

The "why" behind things is what being a lead is all about. The reasons we do things add up to a larger goal or purpose. When we answer the why behind everything we do for a team, we are building a picture of our ultimate goals for the team.

If we've done it right, the team will understand and make decisions based on the purpose we've identified and we won't have to direct them. They will see the direction and move because they want to, not because they were told. If there's a reason they don't want to go in a particular direction, it is also the lead's responsibility to help them understand why and to be flexible enough to take into account what the team member wants.

As a lead, we have to adjust and adapt by listening to the team and giving them ownership. If we can't, for some reason, we need to be able to get the reasons across, to help the team understand why we can't do what they'd rather do. If we are successful, then there is no directing; the why ultimately provides direction without directing.

Firing a Team Member

Likely the hardest thing that any lead will have to do is tell someone that they don't make the cut or can't be on the team anymore. Depending on the work environment, some places are quick to fire, while other places would never fire anyone.

We have to balance this, knowing that both firing a team member and keeping a bad team member is a failure on our part. If we fire a team member, it means we were not able to get them up to speed, get them motivated, or work our goals into their goals. When we keep a bad team member, we are not holding them accountable and setting a bad example for the rest of the team.

Having clear expectations and ensuring everyone is consistently held accountable to those expectations is the answer. Make sure we've done our best to work with their strengths and weaknesses or find more appropriate responsibilities. We have to clearly tell them the things we need them to do and work on, give them an explicit time frame to improve.

Culture and Complaints

The way we praise, the way we criticize, the type of gossip we allow and how we interact daily molds the culture of the team. Whether it is intentional or not, the leaders naturally drive culture on a team. If we stay in the office for 12 hours a day, we are building a culture of staying late, even if it isn't our intention. If we answer emails at home after hours, we are building a culture of being online outside of work.

Ignored or improperly addressed complaints similarly end up having a significant impact on culture. If a squeaky wheel gets no oil, everyone hears it and it could have other negative effects. Yet, if we always focus only on the squeaky wheel, we could end up neglecting other areas.

To ensure that we maintain a healthy team culture, complaints have to be consistently addressed. Firstly, complaints should be things we are unaware of. If we were aware, we should have done something about it or already been transparent about what can't be done about it. Secondly, if things we aren't aware of are coming up as complaints (aside from personal issues), we need to improve our awareness. Are we missing certain key inputs? Are we not listening enough? Are we not asking the right questions?

We should be working to cultivate a culture that is transparent and fair, a culture that can talk about real problems but also doesn't prioritize squeaky wheels unless they are supposed to be.

Being Fair Versus Being Two-Faced

One of the biggest issues with complaints is when it's about other team members. When that happens, we can quickly fall into the trap of pitting one team member's perspective over another's. The moment that happens, one of them will lose respect for us. What if both team members are correct? What if something does need to happen?

This is a two-faced trap where we try our best to appeal to both parties, yet by doing so, we end up making it seem as if we aren't fair. For instance, Bob feels disrespected by Sally and we tell Bob, "That's not right; we'll talk to her," then turn around and tell Sally, "Don't worry about Bob. He's just being temperamental." We are being two-faced and the moment that gets out, we lose massive respect.

Instead, be truthful and articulate about what we do or don't agree with. If it's a very sticky situation, why not bring them both together and hash it out together? Although transparency is great, it isn't our place to pass things on that were told to us in confidence, nor is it our place to placate others with white lies.

Privacy Versus Transparency

Disagreements between two team members don't necessarily need to be brought in front of the entire team. Similarly, being transparent doesn't mean we openly berate or criticize one another. Maybe team members want to talk but don't want everyone to know how they feel.

For example, there is no reason to tell Sally that Mary is jealous of her salary. In a case like this, we have to assume that some of the information is going to get out—maybe Mary ends up telling other people about her annoyance. The result could be toxic gossip about Sally and her unreasonable pay.

Although our example is simple, the point is to underscore that transparency is for sharing generalized topics, not for sharing personal details, thoughts, or feelings. With Mary's jealousy about salary, we can first work to understand the general topics: Why and how did Mary agree to her salary in the first place? Has Mary gotten appropriate reviews and/or raises? How does she know Sally is or isn't worth it? How did she learn of Sally's salary? Ideally, these questions will lead to broader ideas that underscore possible issues like clarifying roles, pay scales, or bonuses, fixing the evaluation process, or addressing raises. All of these broader generalized concepts should be transparent so that everyone is on the same page.

Being the Lead

Taking on a lead role can feel daunting, so let's quickly review the key takeaways:

1. Get to know the team individually before ordering them around, if possible. If not possible due to time constraints, keep in mind that we are drawing from the respect bank and we need to pay them back.

2. Establish seamlessly integrated responsibilities for the team. Make sure they understand the why behind everything.

3. Hold team members accountable consistently. That includes letting them go if needed.

4. Resolve conflict by being transparent whenever possible. Don't hold one team member's word over another's. Have them work things out together if needed.

Finally and most importantly, leading others means we give the team ownership, while simultaneously accepting responsibility when things go wrong. In other words, the team members are the reason for success; the leader is the reason for failure.

If taking responsibility for the team's losses and problems is not something we are willing to do, we should not be a lead.

Echo Chamber and Overfitting

When was the last time you followed a group you didn't agree with? When was the last time you made sure to look at counter-arguments when reading the news or social media posts? How about when you're coming to a conclusion? In today's society, the vast amount of information out there can be seriously overwhelming, not to mention wrong or skewed in some way. There are tons of conspiracies and misinformation. Worse still, there are tons of *true* information that can also cause problems if we don't think about the information holistically.

Echo Chamber

If we look at our likes or the groups we follow, the vast majority of us will find that similar beliefs and political views are in those likes and groups. By default, the content we see is going to be mostly from people or groups we already agree with. Similarly, when marketers sell or solicit to us, they take these metrics and tailor their offerings to what we agree with.

This is great for shopping but when it comes time for understanding or learning or communicating with those who don't agree with us, we give ourselves a major disadvantage. To many of us, we wouldn't have it any other way; we don't want to see some random content that is spouting a bunch of nonsense. But if that nonsense includes 40% of a population, we'd be remiss to not at least come to understand the *truth* in their positions. If we only see our own content, our ability to discern what is true becomes difficult (remember the Monty Hall problem we spoke about?).

Garbage In, Garbage Out. Usually...

We can all agree that if we believe or follow wrong or skewed information, that isn't a good thing. We know that with bad directions, for example, finding our way could be difficult. In computer terms, the matter of garbage data in will generally equal garbage data out. Sure, we aren't computers but the information we read daily is very similar. We process and make assessments based on what we take in.

The exception to that rule depends on whether we know it's garbage data or not. If we know that it could be bad data, we can make use of that and learn from it. For example, if a friend named Jake makes a post saying: "The coronavirus is going to wipe out 20% of the population," firstly, why would we believe or not believe his statement? If he were a doctor currently working for the Center for Disease Control (CDC), we'd probably place much more weight in what he's saying, right?

However, if he is a computer technician working at the same company we work for, chances are he doesn't have quite the means to make that claim. How, then, can Jake's potentially bad information help us?

Context, Context, Context

If we want to know how bad the coronavirus is and whether it will wipe out 20% of the population, we definitely shouldn't count on Jake, the IT guy. Yet, what we did learn is that Jake thinks this is the case. That could be relevant, depending on what we want to use this information for. 1) We can use the information to talk to Jake, to relate to Jake. 2) We can determine what sources Jake is using to come to the conclusion. 3) It could help us understand the overall sentiment about the coronavirus situation 4) And on and on...

It may seem obvious but we often forget this when reading posts, articles, or watching the news or YouTube. All bad information can be useful depending on the context. The key is to know or have the idea that the information **could** be bad. If we assume the information is good, then it's going to be garbage in, garbage out. To re-iterate, if we automatically assume information is *good* then what we really have is improperly categorized information, the end result is no different than having bad information.

Healthy Skepticism

Even the word skeptic sounds like a bad thing but the idea is that we should maintain a healthy questioning attitude toward everything. It allows us to make use of the information, whether it's true or not. Healthy skepticism means that it doesn't put us into analysis paralysis and it doesn't have us constantly arguing with others.

Just because we question something doesn't mean we have to be vocal or explicit in our questioning; it also doesn't mean we have to get everything right before making a decision. It means we have to hold in our minds when things are unknown or unsure instead of marking them with good/bad or right/wrong. In fact, we'll come to find that a large majority of observations are never 100% sure bets; they just approach 100% in our experience or understanding. This leads us to how things that are *true* can also cause problems.

Overfitting and Underfitting

Let's imagine that we see a new post every week about a race crime somewhere in the world. It's the same race against another race every time. Assume that the crimes did occur and there's a high probability that the crimes were, in fact, motivated by some form of racism. What if this is the only information we have about crime in general? What invalid conclusions would we draw?

This is underfitting. Imagine having 100 fur-less sphinx cat photos and having to teach a kid or an AI what a cat is based only on those photos? Drawing conclusions from these photos would make skewed results unless we accounted for the limitations. If we increase the variance in our data, it would mean we take in more possibilities. For example, instead of only having fur-less cats, we'd include many other types. Instead of only seeing the race crimes, we'd make sure to acknowledge all the other non-race crimes to have a balanced perspective.

The slightly harder concept to understand is overfitting. It refers to taking in information that has high variance and low ability to identify trends from the information. Instead of teaching fur-less cats, imagine we wanted to teach the kid or AI 100 distinct animal species from 100 photos. There would be lots of variance because every photo is of something completely different, but having only one instance of dog and one instance of cat could make it hard to delineate from all the other 98 animals. They wouldn't be able to tell why a hyena isn't a dog. Initially they would depend completely on our explanation until we gave them ways to identify trends.

Similarly, what about if we were to decide what's best for our country's national security? With so many factors, it can be difficult to draw conclusions ourselves. We naturally default to an authority or other subject matter expert to tell us what we should know, what trends we should look for and what we should conclude. When we can't identify valid trends on our own and depend on what we've been told, we are encountering overfitting to an extent.

Anti-Echo

With the massive amount of information in the world, it makes sense to look for and listen to experts, authorities and even the echo chambers. They can at least provide us with ways to find and identify trends for ourselves. We just need to make sure to constantly branch out and balance the information we receive. If we don't, we could become underfit and unable to draw valid conclusions or overfit and subject to what others say without even knowing it.

In both cases, we could slowly become extremists, holding very specific truths that cannot create reasonable generalizations. We have to realize that individual pieces of information used to form a generalization may all be true but the generalization itself by definition is only an approximation. The better we balance the information we receive, the better our ability to generalize.

Let's take the time to open our minds to other truths:

1. Join a social media group that is a large part of the population, but one we disagree with.

2. Remember that bad information can be useful and

3. Remember that even 100% true information can yield skewed results.

Divine Intervention
and Luck

There have been accounts of people who have lived after falling out of an airplane or another height that reached terminal velocity, or the fastest speed something can fall with just gravity. How is this even possible when people die after falling out of a two-story building? Of course, we can explain it away with tons of reasons, like foliage, snow, or soft ground broke their fall. But the chances are so slim that it makes us wonder how lucky can someone get? This is a taboo subject, so please keep an open mind and understand that opposing ideas and beliefs can coexist.

What is luck? Typically, we call something luck when we either get something good or bad that was not expected. We generally use it when things are mostly outside of our control. For example, winning the lottery is good luck and being hit by lightning is bad luck.

But what if we found out through years of research that there was a flaw in the lottery pattern and we were able to exploit that pattern? Would that still be good luck? What if we were standing on a tall building, leaning on a lightning rod during a thunderstorm? Would that still be bad luck? Most likely not. In both cases, our choices were a major factor in the outcome.

The thing is, just by adding a little more to these scenarios, we can make them feel more (or less) than just luck. What if the person who got hit by lightning deliberately ran someone off the road because of road rage a few minutes earlier? They got home, got out the car and BAM, got struck by lightning. That could still be considered bad luck but the fact that they just did something bad makes it feel a lot more like divine intervention.

To make it sound like a coincidence, we just need to add some more information. If chances of getting struck by lightning in the U.S. are one in 700,000, that means roughly 460 people get struck by lightning every year. That's more than a person every day. If only five of those 460 people were bad and recently did something wrong, then getting struck by lightning after doing something bad would seem much more like a coincidence than divine intervention.

Why Does This Matter at All?

The mind is a crazy thing. Whenever we call something luck or divine intervention, there's one thing they have in common: the event was outside of our immediate control. If we controlled it to any reasonable extent, it would be like the guy leaning on the lightning rod in a thunderstorm; it wouldn't be luck, it would be clearly in his realm of responsibility.

When we see things as not in our control, we cannot take full responsibility for any of the events that transpire as a result. Further, if we consistently believe things that are false or not repeatable and measurable, we risk developing a mentality that doesn't have strong roots. If someone is struck by lightning and we write it off as bad luck, then there is nothing to be gained from the situation — no lessons, just crap luck. This is a slippery slope because we will never really know.

If we were a caveman or cavewoman standing in a large open field during a lightning storm, we might see getting hit as just bad luck. If we never look at the possibility that it's within our control to an extent, we would never learn to do something about it.

Divine Intervention

Divine intervention is a little different because, in many cases, if we believe something is divine, then we may or may not claim to apply a specific reason to that intervention. For example, if we believe the man who ran someone off the road and got struck by lightning was divine intervention, then we are correlating doing something bad with a form of punishment. That becomes a catalyst to not do bad things ourselves. However, even though the result may be good, we can't claim to know the reason for divine intervention; we can only assume.

That assumption is fine when it deals with a random bad guy getting struck by lightning. However, the assumption can be dangerous if we are using it to determine who should be arrested. For example, "He was struck by lightning, so he must have robbed the bank." To make matters worse, if divine intervention was a real-time, consistent occurrence, would we need police? If we claim to know the specific reasons for divine intervention, we are walking in a sea of assumptions that may be correct but cannot be verified. Logically, they are a series of inductive and abductive reasoning. These are all assumptions that could be wrong and we would never know because we can't accurately repeat and measure the results.

For these assumptions to be proven, they would need other proof or facts to lean on. In religious circles, these facts and proof are often sacred texts, like the Bible. This all, however, is built on an entire area of unknown, requiring that we tread carefully.

An Optimal Perspective

If we encounter good luck, then we need to work hard to determine how we can make it NOT luck in the future. We don't want to depend on good luck; we want our actions to have our own positive influence. If we encounter bad luck, then we need to assume that it's not luck at all and work hard to figure out what could have been done better.

For divine intervention that results in some form of punishment, we can learn from it and take the punishment as a lesson to not do bad actions. However, because it's divine, we can only assume or have faith that we know what we did wrong. But what if it was an accident and we didn't do anything wrong? How would we know? If divine intervention always held everyone accountable, we would not need laws and police. It would be more reasonable to assume that divine intervention is not a standard occurrence and operate as if it did not happen.

Good things that happen due to divine intervention are similar. If we believe that something good has happened because of divine intervention, we can be thankful and continue to do whatever it is that we believed caused the good grace. However, if we assume the wrong thing, we are liable to create cognitive dissonance or conflicts of reality in our minds.

Ideally, even if we believe in divine intervention, we must attempt to take responsibility for everything in our lives because we will never truly know when (or how) intervention is occurring and when it is not.

SOCIETY

"If I knew something that could serve my nation but would ruin another, I would not propose it, for I am first a man ... and only accidentally am I French."
-Montesquieu

Capitalism and Competition

Imagine you are an athlete. You are claimed to be the greatest in the world, the greatest of all time, the GOAT. You've won more championships and set more records than everyone else and you are still in your prime. But recently, you found out there is an extremely good challenger. You've watched their videos and it looks like they copied your style and added their own flair. But they are better if they are as good as those videos indicate. You will probably lose if you compete against them right now. Instead of competing with them, you decide you need to work on yourself to improve before going toe to toe. You change your schedule such that you only compete in areas or divisions that your rival isn't competing in while you improve. If you don't want an L on the record books, it sounds like the only real option: to improve yourself until you are ready to step back into the ring and compete with your rival. Or is it?

China seems to be that rival to the U.S. Trump tweeted about China being of no help and that "Our great companies are ordered to immediately start looking for an alternative to China, including bringing your companies HOME." What isn't being properly addressed or explained is that it looks like we are failing to compete, or even that America is losing at least one competition and as a result, Trump gives an order to business owners to force business to stay in America. Suffice it to say, there are a few logical reasons for more tariffs but does competition have anything to do with it?

Why would a capitalistic country impose rules that ultimately limit competition? Does limited competition promote growth? Doesn't that go against the whole point of competition, almost like being more focused on the winning record than the actual skills and abilities in a sport? In boxing, it's like the champion choosing not to fight a certain fighter because of the high risk of losing; they duck the fight and make it look like it's for other reasons.

The Greatest Competitors in Sports, the GOATs

Can you imagine Michael Jordan or Kobe Bryant ducking a chance to go head-to-head in their prime? How about Jack Nicklaus passing up a chance to go against Tiger Woods in their prime? Would Michael Phelps, Usain Bolt, or any other top world-record-breaking athlete even think for a second to not compete against someone else in their prime? Not a chance.

Without a shadow of a doubt, the greatest competitors would look at the competition as a challenge to overcome. A challenge they have dedicated their lives to overcome. They wouldn't ever want to find loopholes or ways to stay number one that aren't direct head-to-head competition. They want to be the best.

Even these great competitors will tell you it's not just about wanting to be the best. Lots of people want to be the best at something but clearly, very few are. It's all about what type of work ethic and dedication they put into being the best. It's about their relentless mentality and self-confidence. These great competitors would never doubt themselves in the final seconds or in a failed moment; they would immediately get back up, look at whatever they've done wrong and attack the problem 200%.

Sports Versus Life

The thing is, in sports, it's just that: a sport. We can't compare a country's well-being or national strategy to competing in sports. Taking a loss as a country could be devastating. Becoming number two would mean the U.S. dollar would take a plunge, stock markets would plunge, and the world's biggest investors would move out.

Why do we love sports so much though? What is it about sports that makes something in us stir? It's the emotions tied to overcoming obstacles, the inner instinct to fight and beat the odds. Adrenaline and various chemical processes in our brains push us to go further and further when we play sports.

We learn from sports that one of the best ways to improve is competition. It doesn't necessarily mean we have to compete directly against others to be the best but we always need a goal line to surpass. If my fastest 100-meter dash is 10.9 seconds and I've never seen or ran with anyone else, I could think that's the limit of my abilities. I could work hard to improve but not see any improvement and think, that must be it. Seeing someone else do it faster could easily prompt more innovation and ideas about what more I can do.

Something feels intrinsically wrong about crippling competition to force businesses to go away from China. Not only is it against true capitalistic mentality, which America has always pushed as the best way to grow a country but it's against what anyone who is simply a competitor would say is reasonable. For better or worse, tariffs aren't always about competing with China or even crippling them.

Tariffs Are About Collecting Money

If businesses are going to China, it's because they are winning in those areas. They are bringing in money. It's because they are creating products for less cost and they have more people organized to provide labor at a lower wage. There is more land available and their economy has been growing so rapidly that many investors have seen extreme growth in their investments. Easily over **500 billion** dollars of imports come from China into the U.S. annually (as of 2019).

Perhaps many in America and the world believe that ultimately, businesses won't want to pay the premium for Chinese products and as such, find a new way to get their products. Countries all over the world do this. Everyone is looking at ways to keep money and business internal, such that they maximize their profitability.

Passing the Buck to Consumers

The logic appears sound but let's take a real-world example to expose this a little better. Let's use a simple example of importing shirts. If the U.S. raises tariffs on shirts from China, the prices of shirts in the U.S. go up; why is this? A business has three main options: find a U.S. supplier, find a supplier in another country, or pay the extra for a Chinese supplier.

The U.S. suppliers could get a lot more business, possibly driving their costs down a bit but the cost difference is often extreme. For example, I've recently been quoted around three dollars a shirt by a few Chinese suppliers versus nine dollars a shirt from the cheapest U.S. suppliers. This is for good quality material, screen-printed, or sublimation shirts. That means a tariff of 300% would be required to make up that difference. That won't happen, guaranteed. The worst-case scenario is likely something around 25% for shirts/clothing, not nearly enough to justify paying nine dollars a shirt versus a new $3.75 a shirt.

The second option is to find a supplier in another country, not China. The next inexpensive countries are often somewhere in the middle, $5-7 a shirt—closer to competing with China but still not winning. There are a few suppliers in other countries that can compete (but not many). All that means is that most businesses will likely continue to do what they've been doing: buy from China, increase shirt costs and accept the possible sales hit due to a 75-cent uptick in cost to the customer. It happens all the time and customers eat costs like that daily, with very little impact on businesses. Customers pay tariffs ultimately.

Trump knows this. Policymakers know this. Businesses know this. So, what's the real story? What is going to happen to China versus America? Absolutely nothing or very little will happen to China, at least if we're talking shirts. Maybe some other random country can squeak out more business because of it.

The U.S. is going to collect **billions** of dollars due to the tariffs, all money that is actually taken from the American people and the businesses. It's like more taxes before taxes, covered to look like innovative, competition-based issues. It feels less and less to do with competition, capitalism, or GOATs, for better or worse. Instead, it feels more like collecting money to pay off debt or fund new initiatives and spread to the people but at the same time sold to the people.

Right or Wrong

It's not right or wrong as far as the decision to impose tariffs. There are valid reasons for both. What is wrong, however, is that the real reason behind the tariffs and what is happening feels obscured. We tend to use partial truths to validate or confirm our biases. We see things often in right versus wrong, and the media and politicians know this and use it to serve their own agendas.

Technically, China could see an impact due to the tariffs. Maybe a small number of businesses will go elsewhere or come back to the U.S. Maybe a small number of businesses will innovate. But *all* of the story should be told to the people, not simply "bring business home to the U.S." or "we don't need China." We need tweets to also say, "we will earn billions with these new tariffs" and "you may see an increase in prices in your products" and "you, the people, are helping us pay these tariffs until U.S. businesses can do better".

I guess that's too much for any politician to say. We, the people, are partly to blame. We get frustrated at the mention of something that is contrary to our beliefs and will quickly "boooo" them off the stage. We can't tolerate that often, up to half of the population disagree with us on just about every subject and can't see the partial truths or positive aspects of what they believe.

It starts with us—let's do better as a whole and ultimately hold ourselves and everyone else accountable to a higher standard of open tolerance and understanding. Accept disagreement and contrary opinions with open arms and don't see them as a moral right or wrong or a threat to your person or ideology.

Raising Prices in Crisis

You're out of toilet paper and soap. When you get to the store, you realize the shelves are just about empty. It's somewhat of a crisis since a virus is forcing everyone to stay home and hunker down as much as possible. When you finally find a place that has soap and toilet paper, you notice that they're multiple times the normal cost. We generally accept that business is business and let it go, pick up the toilet paper and move on. Fairness and morality aside, does raising prices in this situation make good business sense?

Supply and Demand

Traditionally, economics would tell us that an increase in demand means prices should go up. Because of this dynamic, businesses should similarly raise prices if demand increases. The logic is to just use a simple formula: (price of goods x goods sold) – cost of goods and expenses = profit.

This means increasing the price or the number of goods sold is the bottom line. What if our inventory is somewhat fixed? Then the only tangible things we can change are to either increase the price or decrease the cost of our goods or our expenses. This is Business 101. If we tripled the price of goods during the crisis and sold the same or more than normal, we'd have amazing profits over the course of the crisis. Then we could use this profit to build the business and invest or do whatever it is we wanted to do.

The problem with this model is that it is over-simplistic. It doesn't account for psychological games and manipulation. It doesn't account for how or why customers will continue to buy things in the future. It doesn't account for how competitors will react or try to manipulate things. It doesn't account for how the Internet and social media could react. It doesn't account for the fact that cheating and stealing are very similar (and not in a moral sense).

Cheating and Stealing

There are studies out there that show that, when we aren't thinking about morals, we, "the collective we," have a tendency to cheat a little. For example, giving college students an exam and allowing them to write down their own score produces many cheaters. Now, I promised that we wouldn't use morals as a basis; so, what we want to do is think of cheating and stealing in terms of opportunity, cost and the end goal. If we are provided an exam and we cheat when instructed to write down our own score, our end goal is most likely to get a good score on the exam, get a good grade and get our degree or whatever piece of paper we are trying to get.

However, what if our end goal was to understand our level of knowledge? What if our end goal was to know how we ranked next to our peers? What if our end goal was to be the best for ourselves and not for others, not for show, not for a grade, not for a piece of paper? Would we still cheat? Stealing is no different; it's all based on our end goal.

What we don't like to acknowledge is that cheating and stealing can be logical, given a specific end goal. If we just want an easy, good grade and the teacher is giving us an easy way to cheat and there's no significant chance of it affecting anyone negatively, then it's a no-brainer. Cheat.

The question is, however, are we really assessing the situation correctly? Have we properly identified the risks and impacts to ourselves and others?

Gaming the System

When we find legal loopholes or tricks to get extra out of something or get away with things that weren't meant to be, we're gaming the system. For example, shamelessly, still to this day, when I use a vending machine, I will strategically look for an item that was stocked incorrectly, giving a chance of two for one. The result is essentially stealing from the vending machine owner.

If I was an excellent magician and used sleight of hand to steal a candy bar from a real person, how is it different? Again, right and wrong aside, the only real difference is that one situation is direct, while the other is more of a loophole and indirect.

Yet even if I was caught by a police officer getting two items for one from the vending machine, despite it being stealing, it's not treated the same as directly pocketing a candy bar from the shop.

The point is that we wouldn't normally assess them as having the same amount of risk or impact. In an obviously direct stealing scenario, even if we were a magician, there's a higher risk and higher impact if something went wrong.

Gaming the system is often put in the moral gray area and not treated quite the same as something like direct stealing and is usually legal. Sometimes, it may actually be important to take advantage and game the system, yet the assessment of what risks and impacts it could have is just as important.

Back to Business

In business, the moral gray area of gaming the system is the norm. For example, in corner markets and negotiable stores, they can and will charge as much as possible. If we look rich or like a tourist, the price will get hiked up if they can get away with it.

Given the goal of immediate profit, these tactics are no different than raising prices in crisis. Yet, what are the true risks and impacts? If we aren't going to be in business anymore, then we could logically conclude that making a quick profit by increasing prices makes sense. We won't have to worry about whether customers like us or not; we wouldn't care about social media or Yelp reviews. We'd get our profit and go do whatever we wanted to do with the profit.

This short-term thinking of just getting profits is a normal working business model that has been in place for generations. We've been taught over and over that it's all about the bottom line. Yet why is it that 50% of businesses fail in the first five years? Our societies may have been doing business for generations but with a 50% failure rate, maybe we're doing something wrong.

We're so focused on revenue and profit over our competitors that we forget the whole point of the business: to provide something of value to the customer. Increasing prices in times of crisis is the opposite of providing value to the customer. It's saying, "We know you need this right now, but we want more money, so we're going to get over on you."

Redefining Profit Without Being Non-Profit

If we use the concept of provide value to the customer, then times of crisis are a great time to show the customer how much they are valued and appreciated. In turn, for example, the marketing campaign that normally would have taken lots of money and would provide no immediate value becomes a means to provide value and market at the same time. We could reduce the prices or give away free essential items and not only provide value but also get more loyal customers. The long-term impact could be much more than short-term gains of raising prices.

There are always innovative ways to create value without focusing on increasing the profit margin and the more we do so, the more likely our business will thrive.

Tough Business

The doubters that say the business will also be in jeopardy during times of crisis and say taking as much profit as possible is important fail to see that, if the business cannot afford to weather a crisis, then either 1) The business did not save or plan for bad times. 2) The business started prematurely. 3) The crisis is exposing the fact that the business is not really needed. 4) The doubters are right and the crisis is extreme, except in this instance, raising prices is not going to be the difference-maker.

This is no different than personal financial planning. If we personally aren't at least somewhat prepared for bad scenarios, then we shouldn't be starting a business or taking on a family for that matter. This is a tough pill to swallow but it should be underscored that we all need to work on constantly improving for both ourselves and those we care for. For businesses, that means the employees and the customers.

Hard Times and Crisis

Next time we see a business raise prices in crisis, let's give our business to someone else if we can. There are at least 100 better ways to make money than to take money from others against their will or better judgment. It's a business's job to find those 100 ways or get put out of business.

In hard times, we often see the worst in people. With business, it is no different. It's up to every one of us to hold each other, the businesses and even our own governments accountable. Let's all remember: if we see something wrong, say something. Have discourse without blame. Let's find better solutions together.

Censorship: A Failure?

Freedom is something that most, if not all, of the top countries strive to underscore. Any good business will also do its best to ensure the same. Some unfortunate censorship trends have been happening over the Internet and we are entering a very "touchy" realm that we have to be mindful of. As much as we don't like Facebook censoring users, they have every right to do so, just as we have every right to use another platform.

The justice warriors out there sometimes go a little extreme, using freedom of speech as an excuse to berate others. They want to push laws or require Facebook to not censor users, which would be taking a different freedom away from Facebook and the owner(s).

As always, we need some healthy gray area. We do not want to censor anything. However, are their situations that could arise that influence our decision to censor? Maybe.

The Scenario

Imagine you are in a restaurant with your family. You have a couple of kids from 3–5 years old. Someone comes into the restaurant and sits next to you all and starts talking about how they hate your race. The person looks at you and says, without being angry or intimidating, with a more of a matter-of-fact voice, "No offense but your race just sucks. You all probably don't even know how to begin to be better." You analyze the situation and figure something needs to be said. So, also in a matter-of-fact voice, you say, "No offense but I think you may need to see a psychologist." You hoped the interaction would fizzle so you could continue with your dinner, but, of course, the person continues with more banter about why your race sucks. You ask the person if they could just let it be so you can enjoy your meal but they won't stop. The person is not being outright nasty but it's very annoying and they clearly want to get their point across. You instead ask the staff if you could be moved to another table and you finally part ways with the annoying person. "All's well that ends well," you think and continue on with your meal and time with the family.

Now imagine a slightly different scenario where the berating, annoying person decides to amp up their emotions, gets angry and frustrated, starts to curse and says the most obscene things you can think of to your kids. They don't look like they plan to get up and fight but they are one gesture away from it. They won't stop yelling and saying nasty, disrespectful things about you and your kids. You, of course, would want to do some pretty nasty things to this person too. Things likely won't end well, no matter how much in the right you are.

We Don't Want to Hear It All

And so, we enter censorship. Even with the first scenario, people have a tendency to want to censor. However, since the person wasn't being overtly nasty or provoking, there's no reason to have them removed or censored. They may be racist but they are entitled to their opinion and to express that opinion. Clearly, they should have better manners and read the situation to know that was not the time or place but nevertheless, censoring is not necessary.

However, in the second situation, it is becoming more extreme; emotions are clearly getting evoked. Is it a tougher decision about censorship? What's the difference? Despite what we see as vastly different, it's much more difficult to discern where the line is. Some will want to draw the line at cursing but it's not simply cursing. Others will want to draw the line at the obscene things said about you and your kids. Would you want them to be censored if possible in that situation? If you could, would you press a button to not have to hear them spew whatever obscenities cross their mind?

Perspective Matters

One aspect we haven't addressed yet is perspective, which is a strong differentiating factor affecting this equation. What does "obscene" mean? What does "angry and frustrated" mean? What is "cursing"? What does someone look like when they are about to fight or threaten you? What does "disrespectful" mean? Why does it matter that they were angry or frustrated? And who is this "person"?

The point is, to some, cursing is the norm and so the vast majority of cursing would not be considered "obscene." For others, talking about sex is obscene. For some, physical harm is a very fast next step after these obscenities. While for others, it would take much more.

The thing is, it is imperative to understand that 100 different people could answer all of those questions in 100 different ways. The who for some people is also significant to determine the need for censorship. If the person was a seven-year-old boy versus a 30-year-old man versus a 30-year-old person with a mental disorder, would they all get censored the same?

Should they? Who can answer these questions and how can we have the audacity to say we know the best answer for the masses?

How are we supposed to determine what is censored when everyone has such vastly different ways of interpreting what should or shouldn't be censored? This is sounding more and more like it isn't our call and as such, we have to say no to censorship, no matter how berating and annoying. Although we don't agree with Facebook censorship, we empathize and understand how difficult it would be to try and walk that line.

Enter Filtership

We have no desire to censor but we also know that there are things out there that we don't want to see or hear about. Having some form of "filtership" is something that we would love to see incorporated everywhere instead of forms of censorship—something akin to covering up a spoiler and the over-18 tags. If you want to see the content that is flagged, you have to select it deliberately through a filter. That way, we don't have to censor; we could just move to another room.

Let's all help promote ways to never censor things if at all possible. Will there ever be a time where we truly need to censor something? I don't think so but I acknowledge that:

"Everyone has a plan until they are punched in the face."
-Mike Tyson

Centralized Social Media Must Fail

I registered a Twitter business account recently and proceeded to link it to my website. After putting the site on all of the social platforms and connecting everything together, I started posting. A week later, I thought, "Oh shoot, I still need to update the profile info." So, I uploaded pictures, came up with a cool catchy bio and entered the birthday as the date of company inception. The moment I hit yes, the site locked me out of the account, saying, "Only 13 and older allowed. Please submit a request for review to unlock by uploading a government-issued photo ID to confirm identity."

If I was under 13, I would create another email address and say that I'm 13. What is this actually helping? Does this ensure honest 12-year-olds don't get access to the latest Trump or Kardashian tweets? This feels like it's in place to protect Twitter, the business. It's another terms and conditions, a means of limiting liability if something bad were to happen involving a child. My personal annoyance for being locked out aside, there is something about centralized social media that is a bit worrisome.

Global Means Global

With 195+ countries in the world, that makes a LOT of laws. With over 4,200 religions, that's a lot of possible morals. That is the Internet. There may be a lot of facts, but not everyone agrees with everyone else's facts. We could go with the most restrictive policies but that doesn't work because then we wouldn't even use electricity or the Internet. We could go with the most relaxed policies but then we'd have complete debauchery.

Who is to choose which way is right? No one can choose because there will always be disagreements. This is why filtering is the answer, not censoring. True filtering cannot be done in a centralized construct; there are no laws that can cover these 195+ countries completely. The concept of filtering would be subject to laws in many countries, all of them different.

We normally like large centralized organizations because it provides a level of comfort and accountability. That comfort however, comes with the risk of these organizations having massive power and complete control. Not only that but even the most benevolent global organization is not always truly global in terms of what they promote or represent.

What if instead we could establish a method of accountability at a smaller level? Then, corrupt companies wouldn't be able to stay in power any easier than corrupt individuals. This may sound impossible but the fact is decentralization can push things back to lower levels of control and accountability.

Decentralized Constructs on the Internet

Google, Facebook, Twitter, YouTube, LinkedIn, etc. are centralized constructs. They are controlled by a single organization or by a single governing body that sets rules for the masses. If it's not Twitter's rules, it's laws of the company's home or the rules of the country it is operating in.

However, the decentralized movement is slowly picking up steam. The idea is that we could all own a piece of the Internet that we participate in. We can all own a piece of the social media sites since we are making the content ourselves. The idea is capitalism on steroids or mutated, allowing for even more to succeed and make our unique mark. In traditional capitalism, we have the 1% producing half of the wealth in the world. This is the exact problem socialist and communistic ideals are trying to battle. The problem is that those same ideals give up too many freedoms and assume perfect social scenarios, while forcing those who are in the 1% to share, despite any efforts they made to get to where they are going.

Instead, we need to grow from the old way of thinking. Decentralized ideas, for example, would take a bit from the Googles, the Verizons and the Amazons of the world and make it such that many more pockets of success exist. They would maximize our freedoms, while at the same time, reduce these large organizations control. It's the equivalent of having a farm, a bank and a local market in everyone's backyard and in their own hands.

Evolving Tech

A few things in the tech industry have been interestingly apparent. We've gone back and forth between centralized mainframes to decentralized PCs, back to centralized web environments, to decentralized mobile devices, back again to centralized cloud computing and now we're seeing more decentralized constructs again.

As we evolve, the decentralized constructs get more integrated, more capable. A simple example is our mobile phones. We all have wireless devices with lots of capabilities. In a city, what is the point of having centralized services connecting them all when they could all connect to each other? There are a few reasons we can't easily do this currently but it is not at all outside of the realm of possibility.

The effects of that could be much more far-reaching than we realize. A billion-dollar industry could go back into the hands of the people naturally.

AI in the Room and UBI

With AI on the horizon (note: we disagree with Jeff Bezos, who says AI isn't going to eventually take many of our jobs as we know them today), these decentralized concepts are going to become imperative. We should all have our own ways to make money and survive; the closer we can get to that both digitally and physically, the better.

This means we would not need to push for universal basic income (UBI). We need to put the freedoms into everyone's hands. If we are given UBI, we are continuing to relinquish control to the governments and organizations that manage us. This may seem fine in the top countries but it would be a nightmare for those countries that are less well-off economically or are more corrupt.

What better way to control a population? Once an organization controls our income, what else can they control? What freedoms are we relinquishing that we won't realize until the wrong person or group of people takes power?

We also seem to assume that with no more traditional jobs, we cannot continue to make money. What the loss of traditional jobs should naturally do, however, is change the economy such that we start to pay for different things. It's already happening now; we are getting paid to record ourselves baking cookies, to rant about our own personal problems, to make funny videos. But currently, that pay is still governed by centralized organizations.

Centralized Social Media

Centralized social media must fail because it is very similar to an organization controlling our money on our behalf. Our voices are now heard primarily through social media. While operating this business, I have been blocked at times for unknown reasons on Facebook, Twitter, LinkedIn and Google. While it is most likely these blocks or account lock situations were done in error or have some special requirement, just the fact that it is that easy to silence a voice by the decision of a single organization or entity should not be acceptable.

Social media is amazing, so this has nothing to do with bashing social media. It's all about getting the ideas out there so that we can develop the next iteration of decentralized controls to maximize freedoms everywhere.

Let's try to maintain some level of control and influence individually, to move about freely without being tied to a government or organization to feed us and give us income, without allowing anyone to control our voices. We need to be aware and acknowledge the possibilities; it could save us (or our decedents) in the long run.

20xx Census: Groups Based on Physical Characteristics

You're filling out a form when you come across the ethnicity and race section. You may wonder, "Why do they have Mexican, Latino or other Spanish in the ethnicity selection but no other ethnicities? Why is it that white and black are the only "colors," and the rest seem to be countries/regions? Why is someone from the Middle East considered white? Why is Trump wanting to establish Jewish as a race/ethnicity? Why do we capture race but not religion?" If we really think grouping people based on physical characteristics is useful, why sugarcoat it?

Number of Free People

It's clear we've had our share of failures if we just look at the history of the census. In the U.S., the census seems to have officially started in 1790. We collected the numbers of "Free White Men," "Free White Women," "Free Other," and "Slaves" back in the day. In Virginia for example, they registered 292,627 slaves but 227,071 free white males—clearly a significant population of free to slave ratio. In defense of our forefathers, it makes sense that if the population was made up of primarily one race and a bunch of slaves, we wouldn't need any other distinction. There wasn't really a need to get numbers of "black" or other ethnicities, just slaves or "other free."

It didn't take too long to start to add race categories, however. By 1820, "free colored person" made the list, along with "foreigners not naturalized" and a mention of "Indians not taxed" as well. In fact, they added a third color to the list by 1850: black, white, or "mulatto" for mixed. By 1890, Chinese and Indians got their own letters, finally. By 1890, we really started to get diverse and wanted to know who was "quadroon" or a quarter black. While that did show progress, by 1930, we went back to calling anyone black, no matter how much percentage, a "negro." Similarly, mixed "white and Indian" were to be called "Indian". At this time, we also decided to include "Mexican" as a race (not ethnicity).

What's the Point?

Ok, enough of the crazy history of the U.S. census. As we may have gathered, the point of the census isn't just to have fun with race numbers. It was used to determine how to create laws and policies. It's all about who makes up the country; it's about collecting data. The more data we collect, the more ability we have to tailor our policies and budgets to continue to "improve things as a whole."

The natural downside is that, similar to the "quadroons" out there, the question of whether our "best interests" are at heart is always a fear. With the new executive order for Jews, is it possible that the U.S. Census will have something added to it this year "race/ethnicity-wise"? And what would be the point? We always assume the worst and there's no telling what the various statistics are being used for.

Clearly, there are various budgets and social programs making use of these racial and ethnic statistics. But is that a good thing? And what if the ambiguity of race is causing big mistakes?

Ambiguity of Race

The most recent 2010 census went into detail on various Asian groups, for example, but if we think about it, the census has divided the U.S. into six big groups: Latino-ish, Black-ish, White-ish, Asian-ish, Native-American-ish and Islander-ish. Now how are those metrics really helping? And isn't it a gross difference between a "white" Romanian American that has been here for generations and a "white" Romanian American that came over recently? What about a "black" African American here for generations versus a "black" Ghanaian American that came over recently?

Most would have to agree they represent very different societal factors. The Romanian family who has been here for generations may barely even consider themselves Romanian; their families have possibly all been mixed with various other races and ethnicities by now. Whereas a Romanian just flying in may have a very different outlook. Why wouldn't the census bureau want to capture those details? Instead, we're stuck with two colors (white/black) and everything else.

Ethnicity and Politics

What better way to muddy the water than with a block on "ethnicity" that only singles out "Latino, Mexican and Spanish"? Firstly, ethnicity is a similarly ambiguous social term like race except, instead of focusing on physical characteristics, it focuses on everything else like language, nationality and culture. (Ask a sociologist what culture actually means.) What's the point of having an "ethnicity" but only targeting

Latino-ish folks? Can't we call "African American" an ethnicity more so than a race? Especially considering "Black American" can be significantly different culturally from a "Black Nigerian"?

When we really think about it, all of it just makes it look like a way to get numbers about key political topics. Need a reason to fight for or against immigration and a border wall? Show the growth of "Mexicans" over the last 10 years, adjusted to account for children. The way it is divided today is so unreasonable that the only way it makes sense is to assume it is for political agendas that are believed to be the "best way" to help the U.S.

Slanted Eye and Nose Width Scale?

Some believe that there could be important biological differences between "white" and "black," so therefore it matters. Or that "classification" by "physical characteristics" can reasonably be done. This may have been the case prior to airplanes but the world is becoming a vast melting pot, especially in the U.S.

Since it's so vastly complex, we could allow everyone to select a color palette for their skin color. Then have a round to slanted eye scale; a small to big lip scale and a skinny to wide nose scale. Then we could add the rest of the characteristics, like hair color and eye color. That sounds ridiculous, right? Why do we feel the need to get statistics on "physical characteristics" but sugarcoat it? Back when we were trying to figure out "who is free" versus "who is not," it kind of made sense. But now, what? Is it for college entrance perks? For minority assistance budgets? Jobs and affirmative action?

The bottom line is that classifying someone based on physical characteristics is getting harder and harder except for the purest of racial groups. There may be differences but technology is showing more and more increasingly that if we want to truly identify the differences, we need the genes. Just looking can do but only so much. Of course, most of us would take a hard pass on donating genes for the census.

Most Reasonable Option

Wouldn't it be reasonable to take the race/ethnicity question off altogether? Instead, we could use something to denote where we came from. Something like first, second, third, or more generation American and original country of origin. Then primary and secondary language. That's it. No more tracking quadroons and other racial mixtures. No more switching between colors (white/black) and ethnicity as if it matters.

Then guess what that would mean? Both the well "intentioned" social programs and any discriminatory groups would start focusing on other data collection efforts regarding economics, generational immigration and education—not race. The day we do that is the day we move forward "socially" as a country instead of being held back deliberating over "groups based on physical characteristics."

Privileged

Think back to when you were a child and recall Little Suzie had all the best toys, best clothes and the coolest parties with bouncy houses. You never used to think about the fact that you didn't really have many toys. You didn't think about the fact that you used water in your cereal. You were happy, regardless. Little Suzie and her things, however, started to mess with your head. Through no fault of her own, she had an abundance of treasure that was so awesome. Was Little Suzie privileged? Why does it even matter?

There were other examples of this when you were a child. There was a kid called Little Mike, who was a physical phenomenon — tall, tough and athletic. No one on the playground could compare in any sport. You wished you could run as fast as him or play basketball as well. But no matter how hard you tried, there was no touching Little Mike in sports. He was clearly endowed with a natural ability through no fault of his own.

Why couldn't you eat name-brand Captain Crunch with milk every morning? How come you couldn't get a bouncy house for your birthday party? Why couldn't you get a PlayStation? How come all the kids loved hanging out with Little Suzie but not you? Why couldn't you be cool as Little Mike on the playground? That thinking started a bug in your mind, making you want things you didn't really want or need originally.

Uneven Scales

Many of us want what Little Suzie and Mike have. We want Little Suzie to share more and we either want to be on Little Mike's team or make him play with bad players, so we have a chance. We want things to be more even instead of accepting things as they are and working on ourselves.

We were just kids back then, so likely, our mentality came from our parents or guardians. Did we do everything we could to learn how to be as good as Little Mike? Or did we just complain when he was on the other team? Did we learn to be happy for Little Suzie and focus on things we had more control over, or did we just get jealous?

The uneven scales are like a natural measuring tool. It doesn't seem like the purpose of these feelings is to make us bitter against everyone who is in a better place than us. If anything, it can help us see what we do or don't want in the future; it gives us goals to chase. If we frame it in a good way, we can make the most of it, be happy for Little Suzie and Mike and teach them things they may even see as lucky for us.

Jealousy and Envy

For anyone who can recall a feeling of jealousy at any point in their life, one thing is sure: it is not a good feeling. The body and mind don't want us to continue to be in this state. Just like with anger, the point isn't to stay angry; it's there to re- mind us to do something about our situation. It's our choice to decide what to do about it.

These feelings regarding Little Suzie and Little Mike seem like they come from a place of jealousy. What's more, there's a fine line that separates the more internally focused jealousy from a more externally focused desire for what someone else has. When we start to try and balance things out artificially, when we try and force Little Suzie and Little Mike to our own level due to our internal sense of justice, that becomes the definition of envy.

Now, this isn't to say privileged situations don't exist—they do. And it isn't to say the feelings of jealousy and envy are not allowed or aren't a natural part of life.

The point is that the emotions are there telling us to do something about our situation with respect to **ourselves**, not to do something to Little Suzie or Little Mike. Maybe we should learn to stop comparing. Maybe we should work harder to become better. Maybe we should think of other ways to make more friends. All of these things we do within and for ourselves, not by forcing or taking from others.

Perspective

As we consistently see, everything is a matter of perspective. Little Suzie may have a hard time making friends without resorting to showing off her treasure trove. She may hate that kids love being around her because of her things and not her. Little Mike could get tired of being told he's lucky and that he didn't have to work hard to be a good basketball player.

Of course, in the same vein, maybe they do have it all. Maybe they had great parents that taught them to be humble and thankful, to navigate the social trolls, to stand up for what is right. Why would it matter if they have it all and are doing great? Why not learn from them then? And if they aren't humble, thankful or understanding, why not teach them?

What if, while we were busy always looking at Little Suzie and Mike, there was another kid that lived next door to our apartment. We never thought about him and didn't remember his name but whenever we saw him, he would look over longingly. His mom would always carry him up the steps. It didn't seem like he could walk but we never really thought about it. We just kept thinking about Little Suzie and Mike...

Injustice or Privileged

Generally speaking, in American society, when we hear "privileged," we think about either wealth or racism. But the fact is, as we've seen, it's just another term of comparison, comparing our advantages and disadvantages against others.

This isn't necessarily a bad thing. There have been many times in history where there was injustice toward other groups. Those perpetuating the injustices were the privileged groups. Time and again, rebellions and revolts have occurred to tip the scales to make things more fair.

Questioning potential injustice is a must but when we do, it shouldn't be done by sweeping judgments. Identifying injustice has to be articulate and specific. Ultimately, being privileged in itself is not an injustice.

Privileges will exist in this world and we need to stop using the term to identify injustices. If there's a real injustice, we need to focus on that problem instead of what we think or perceive is the byproduct. If Little Suzie stole to get everything she has, the injustice is that she stole things, not that she is privileged.

Even if Little Suzie not only stole things but also got away with it because of her race, the injustice is still that she stole things and got away, not that she is a privileged race. If an entire race is treated differently in the courts, the injustice isn't that an entire race is privileged, the injustice is that the courts aren't treating everyone properly. This may seem like semantics but focusing on a privileged race instead of fair trials could lead us to take from Little Suzie instead of addressing the actual injustice.

Taking From Little Suzie

Like we've established, Little Suzie had nothing to do with the fact that she was born into a wealthy family. Similarly, no one was born into a particular race, majority, or minority through their own design. It just is.

We may want equality and we may want what Suzie has but should we take from her? Taking Little Suzie's things to give to all the other kids in the neighborhood isn't up to the other kids. It's up to Little Suzie. If Little Suzie is nice, maybe she'll give gifts on her own accord.

Of course, Little Suzie could suck and be mean, not wanting to share, feeling entitled and believing that everyone else is beneath her. Yet in other cases, Little Suzie's friends could suck and be jealous and hateful that she has more than them, wishing the worst for her and leeching off of her any chance they can get. This is similar with racism and many other inequalities in the world. Some people, groups and countries will have more; others will have less. There will be groups that hate other groups and wish them the worst for reasons only they can understand.

The thing is, despite it feeling better to take from someone who is mean, selfish or ignorant, it's still not the way we should do things. We address injustices based on the specific injustice and nothing more. Being mean and selfish isn't an injustice; it's our right to be a jerk. Let's stop trying to force things to be taken from those who are more privileged, even if it may feel good or seem to balance the scales.

Growing from the Crap and Dirt

If we happen to be the underprivileged, we have to acknowledge the hand that life gave us and work from there. We can grow much stronger than anyone who hasn't seen or dealt with the things we have. Focusing on taking things from others is simply envious and will have us quickly forgetting that there is *always* someone who is less privileged than ourselves, guaranteed.

Let's find the energy from the crap and the dirt we came up in. For those who want to be lucky like Little Suzie, we will outwork them. If there's someone who's mean and thinks everyone is beneath them, we will show them through our own mentality that they are wrong.

When we learn to grow from the dirt, from the crap that life throws at us, without being jealous and bitter, we will not only be immensely tough but we'll end up being a pretty awesome person. We will, however, start to develop our own privileges through our hard work and mindset. This isn't a bad thing; it's only natural.

At some point, whether through our own perseverance, mindset, or luck, there is **always** going to be someone less privileged than ourselves. This means we all have a bit of Little Suzie or Little Mike in us. Don't forget where we came from. Always be thankful and make use of any privileges we may have to do positive things for those around us.

Divided We Fall

You are messaging with a friend when you see a series of posts start to flow in about a tragedy that just happened. Before you have time to process what is going on, you see a slew of reactions ranging the spectrum from: "They were asking for it," to "This happens all the time; what's the big deal?"

On and on, we see reactions snap back and forth at each other about who's to blame and who's ignorant, escalating quickly into name-calling and derogatory comments. Why would any potential tragedy turn from that sucks — a bad thing just happened to someone — to blame and belittling remarks?

The Art of Controversy

When misfortune befalls someone, we can always divide it into whether there was foul play or if there was an ability to influence what happened. The more indiscriminate the tragedy, the more we tend to come together. There usually isn't much ability to blame anyone; it just happens. During a natural disaster like a tsunami or an earthquake, we all quickly stand together and help each other out.

Similarly, if someone dies of cancer, most people would be relatively united because it is a hardship for that person and those close to them. Without any other information, there isn't much we can discriminate.

Yet, what if we add the fact that this was an eight-year-old child who wasn't diagnosed until a couple of days before their death? Now, there could be outcries; some might automatically assume that the parents must have been negligent. Others might think that the doctors should have found it earlier. All we have to do to incite unrest is to continue to add factors to the potential disagreements.

What if it happens to be a child of a minority race and there is speculation that the child had fewer options than another child of a different race? What if we have the government and other organizations put in their two cents? One political group is calling for healthcare reform as a result. Another political group is claiming that the proposed healthcare reform will be detrimental to the economy. As things get more heated, a large group of people begins to protest that there needs to be better healthcare for minorities. An opposing group also forms, who are predominantly of the majority race, believe that the media is skewing reality for political agendas.

To create controversy, we have to identify the most emotional topics that gain large-scale attention and then find the facts on opposite ends of the attention. With social media and technology, it's easy to do. Anyone with a few thousand dollars can push a marketing campaign to reach a million people. It doesn't take a conspiracy anymore; anyone can use real-world events and create a nationwide controversy.

Passionate Controversy

By definition, controversy is heated or an emotionally charged, prolonged disagreement between public groups. From the start, once we noted the child was diagnosed only days before their death, our emotions were engaged. Many of us will naturally empathize with the child and the parents. We will wonder, "how the heck could cancer go that long undetected?" We'd hate for that to happen to us or anyone in our family. What was or wasn't done? If foul play could have been involved, that same empathy is going to have us feeling angry or passionate about the outcome.

If these feelings were pointed in the same direction as everyone else, then all would be fine. Yet, once we point passionate feelings against each other, fights and controversy ensue. Once it starts, how often will a passionate person change their mind to agree with the opposition? Just about never.

Useless Facts

In any good controversy, there are plenty of facts on both sides of opposing views. Imagine that, in our scenario, there was a higher instance of deaths due to cancer misdiagnosis for the child's race. That would support the need for reform. However, what if other statistics show that the cancer is harder to detect in that race? Just as we have conflicting beliefs, we almost always have conflicting facts. How are we going to convince anyone that our facts are better than their facts?

With "fake news," propaganda, political agendas, contradicting facts and biased statistics, the result is that we keep believing whatever supports our initial thoughts and feelings. Facebook started putting false information tags on posts, yet they have already been shown to be wrong at times. Opposing groups believe Facebook as a whole is biased and only supports certain political agendas. Even if Facebook was trying to do the right thing, half the population wouldn't believe it. Facts are just about useless when used in a sea of controversy.

Tragedy of Controversy

The worst controversies have some form of injustices riddled within. As we have seen time and again, when injustices occur amidst controversy, it's very difficult to properly address them. If a terrorist or another country wanted to destroy the U.S., all they'd have to do is incite more racial injustices. The straw that breaks the camel's back only takes one more incident, by one more person.

Now that all of these passionate disagreements are spinning around, guess who is practically left alone in the eye of the storm? The memory of the eight-year-old who passed away is practically trampled on. While everyone is focused on the agendas of others, the opposition and the differences between what did or didn't happen and the injustices, those who are the closest end up swept away in controversy.

What truly matters? How do we cut through all the noise of controversy? When we can't agree on what the injustice is, at least on a fundamental level, there will always be controversy.

Baseline Agreement

Even though there are lots of useless facts circling, there will always be a root level concern that the vast majority would agree with. This is the only hope we have for a united front. Without the ability to lean on facts or the open-mindedness of people, we are left with very few options. We have to go back to the essence of what happened. In our case, an eight-year-old died of cancer. That is the tragedy that everyone can agree on. That is our baseline agreement.

From there, we can expand the agreement by just a little

more: None of us wants that to happen to other children. And a little more: We want doctors to be able to diagnose things well in advance whenever possible. Once we establish that very first baseline agreement, other small areas will start to be identified, creating more understanding.

Going to the baseline can help identify the deeper problems as well. For example, although it is obvious today, in the matter of slavery, a baseline agreement could be: Innocent people shouldn't be owned by others like property and forced to obey. That baseline agreement would underscore the problem: Slaves weren't considered innocent people. However, the moment that is proven to be possible, the controversy starts to fall apart.

The problem is that once we go too far or make decisions based on those agreements, we quickly enter back into the controversial realm. Everyone has different opinions about how to make things happen. If it's a big enough topic, there won't be one good answer.

No matter what passionate beliefs we have about what did or didn't happen, what should have happened, or who is to blame, we must find and hold very firmly in our minds as many baseline agreements as we can.

United We Stand

We will never fully agree on any major topic and that's completely ok; everyone is entitled to their own opinions and really, that's a good thing. We just need to be reminded that the more we get caught up blaming others or casting aspersions, we become the reason for controversies and large-scale disagreements. When we individually divide ourselves from each other, our societies start to do the same, resulting in major conflicts and disputes that end in more tragedy.

The essence of standing together means we tolerate the differences. Our differences can be very easy to tolerate if we find the baseline agreements. If we do this well, we can learn to disagree with class and respect. We can have engaging conversation and discourse even when we disagree.

Intolerance and a divided front are the essences of every fight, every war and every fallen nation. Let's remind anyone who is getting caught up in passionate debates over tragedies that there is just about always a baseline we all can agree on. Let's focus on that and treat one another the way we would treat our loved ones.

P.S.

I wrote this because of various posts I've seen regarding George Floyd (rest in peace). Race and police brutality have been long-time controversies in many countries. No matter what you believe about George, about the police involved, about race issues, about political agendas or any conflicting facts, remember to find the baseline agreements.

The sobering truth is that another injustice WILL happen even as we make great progress. It's not reasonable to expect a race crime to never happen again, just as it is not reasonable to expect a murder to never happen again. Let that really sink in. If we make improvements, if we start to move toward a common understanding, one hateful person could perform a targeted crime and we're right back where we started. We must control reactions and put them in perspective.

Let's stop there, be tolerant and remember to stand together despite our disagreements and differences.

Epilogue

You may have noticed that no matter what the topic, a few key concepts always seem to crop up. Let's go through them and recap the lessons.

Context and Perspective

A great reminder of context and perspective is that one plus one literally isn't always two. Your perspective may be different from someone else's perspective, and yet both of you could be right. To navigate life, we have to be able to see other perspectives. To do so, we need to take in as much non-biased information about the particular situation as we can. In other words, we need to build and understand the context surrounding situations so that we can have a holistic perspective.

Cognitive Dissonance and Fallacies

Nothing seems to be a bigger problem in navigating problems and situations than our own way of thinking. We can spin our own web of self-deception in a blink of an eye and have no problem believing it without any doubt. No one is safe from the grips of cognitive dissonance and logical fallacies. The best we can do is never stop proving ourselves wrong. We have to treat everything with healthy skepticism, especially the beliefs entangled with strong emotion.

Communication and Boundaries

Relationships or interpersonal interactions are a fact of life. We must interact, yet we have a vast network of thoughts and beliefs that cannot all be communicated perfectly. There will be misunderstandings. There will be disagreements. There will be times when no one is right, or everyone is right. Being able to communicate adequately with each other requires that we establish our boundaries so that everyone knows our own perspectives and context.

Comparison and Social Influences

We are very weak to social influences. From the day we are born, we are comparing ourselves to others to determine how we should act and what we should learn. Then, without any real guidance, we are supposed to either stop comparing ourselves or only allow ourselves to be influenced by just the right people. Unfortunately, it isn't an on-off switch, and so we fight with unreasonable social influences all our lives. Improving our own self-confidence and self-awareness is crucial to battling this.

Managing Emotions

Almost everything that becomes difficult in our lives is wrapped up in emotions, so much so, that we lose sight of what is actually difficult. Is it the emotions that are difficult, or is it the situation that brought about the emotions? My belief is that emotions are our alarm system, based on our own needs and desires. Solving the situation almost always solves the emotions as well. When that isn't quite enough and we're still overly emotional, there is a good chance we need to refocus our overarching goals.

Establishing Goals

The clichés about goals are usually true. The ship without a destination will drift endlessly, randomly. Unless we want random chaos in our lives, the best idea is to plot out a course by establishing unyielding goals. Have direction and take out the compass to make sure you're heading the right direction every single day.

Embracing Mistakes and Failure

None of the areas mentioned above can be done well without being ok with making mistakes and failing. The fear of failure has debilitated countless people from moving forward, from doing things they should do. Embracing failure doesn't mean we are supposed to be reckless; it means that we will always put our everything, our sweat, blood, and tears into something, knowing we may not succeed.

Thank You!

This wasn't a specially curated list; it was just an interesting, unintended result. It seems that if we ultimately learn to navigate these areas well, we can handle the majority of what life throws at us.

If anything resonated with you or if you didn't like something in particular, send me a note with your thoughts directly to kira(at)failfection.com.

This publication is original work licensed under Creative Commons Attribution-ShareAlike.

Thank you for reading Failfection: Life and Lessons.

Bibliography

Antonopoulos, Andreas M. *The Internet of Money. A Collection of Talks.* Merkle Bloom LLC, 2017.

Ariely, Dan. *Predictably Irrational: The Hidden Forces That Shape Our Decisions.* Harper Perennial, 2010.

Becker, Gavin De. *The Gift of Fear: Survival Signals That Protect Us from Violence.* Bloomsbury, 2010.

Chapman, Gary D. *The 5 Love Languages.* Northfield Pub., 2015.

Collins, James C. *Good to Great.* Random House Business, 2001.

Covey, Stephen R. *The 7 Habits of Highly Effective People.* Franklin Covey, 1998.

Csikszentmihalyi, Mihaly. *Flow: The Psychology of Optimal Experience.* Harper Row, 2009.

Dörner Dietrich. *The Logic of Failure: Recognizing and Avoiding Error in Complex Situations*. Basic Books, 2010.

Dyer, Wayne W. *Your Erroneous Zones*. Avon, 1976.

Fabry, Joseph B. *The Pursuit of Meaning: A Guide to the Theory and Application of Viktor E. Frankl's Logotherapy*. Beacon Press, 1968.

Goggins, David. *Can't Hurt Me: Master Your Mind and Defy the Odds*. Lioncrest Publishing, 2019.

"How Many People Have Ever Lived on Earth?" *Population Reference Bureau*, 24 Aug. 2018, www.prb.org/howmanypeoplehaveeverlivedonearth/.

Huff, Darrell, and Irving Geis. *How to Lie with Statistics*. W.W. Norton & Co., 2006.

Lewis, H. W. *Why Flip a Coin?: The Art and Science of Good Decisions in Everyday Life*. Wiley, 1998.

"List of Countries by Life Expectancy." *Wikipedia*, Wikimedia Foundation, 2020, en.wikipedia.org/wiki/List_of_countries_by_life_e xpectancy.

Neurocritic. "What is a Thought." *The Neurocritic*, 2017, neurocritic.blogspot.com/2017/06/what-is-thought.html.

Ramachandran, V. S., and Sandra Blakeslee. *Phantoms in the Brain: Probing the Mysteries of the Human Mind.* Harper Perennial, 2009.

Sapolsky, Robert M. *Behave: The Biology of Humans at Our Best and Worst.* Penguin Books, 2018.

Index

Made in the USA
Middletown, DE
08 September 2020

17909386R00161